NAVIGATING CHANGE

a FIELD GUIDE *to* PERSONAL GROWTH

by W. GARY GORE

Published by Team Trek. First Edition published 2002.

Designed by Disciple Design

ISBN 0-9656506-6-5

ACKNOWLEDGMENTS

It is impossible to cover all those persons who have influenced my thinking and view of life as put forth in this book. There are, however, key persons -- friends, colleagues, family, and, certainly, writers whose work I have enjoyed and absorbed over the years. I would like to acknowledge these.

At the top of this list are Team Trek clients who have pushed me out of my comfort zone and challenged me to grow with them. Among this group of many are Steve Nielsen, Ed Champagne, Frank Thomas, Mark Godbold, Mark Daniel, Karen Langham, Roy Smith, and my partner Jack Meyer. Our clients have simply been the driving force in our continuing to grow in all that we do.

No list would be complete without the name of my pastor, Dr. Adrian Rogers, who has opened the word of God to my eyes and heart. Writers who have influenced me greatly are James Allen, Dr. Larry Crabb, Viktor Frankl, Dr. Stu Weber, Coach John Wooden, Anne Morrow Lindbergh, Charlie Plumb, Peter Senge, Oswald Chambers, C. S. Lewis, and Daniel Goleman. There are many others.

Most important is my wife, Lori, who is my soul mate, friend, colleague, accountability partner, and, yes, my sandpaper. She simply makes me want to be a better man, to reach for higher possibilities, and do everything with excellence.

And, finally, my incredible family: mother Maxine, sons Jeff, Mike, and Craig, daughters Kim, Katie, and Liz, and five wonderful grand-children.

TABLE OF CONTENTS

THE CRUCIBLE

Success is not measured by what a person accomplishes, but by the opposition they have encountered, and the courage with which they have maintained the struggle against overwhelming odds. Opposing circumstances create strength. Opposition gives us greater power of resistance. To overcome one barrier gives us greater ability to overcome the next. It is defeat that turns bone to flint, and gristle to muscle, and makes us invincible, and formed the heroic nature that is now in ascendancy in the world. Do not, then, be afraid of defeat. You are never so near to victory as when defeated in a good cause.

- Henry Ward Beecher

The warriors in the elite U.S. Special Forces are as close to super heroes as you are likely to find. Only the finest and toughest are invited to compete for a few hundred positions, and they undergo the most rigorous physical and psychological training imaginable. As an integral part of this training, they will march for miles through swamp, forest, mountains, and deserts using only a topographical map and compass to navigate. Food rations are limited, and every conceivable adversity is thrown at them to assess their ability to handle stress, ambiguity, and change.

The U.S. Marine Corps concludes its basic training with a three-day cross-country march in which participants are deprived of sleep and food and are subjected to all manner of stressful situations. Why? The purpose of this type of training is to equip a warrior with the skills necessary to survive and thrive in the most adverse conditions possible. This final phase of Marine Corps training is a test called The Crucible. It is an apt name and certainly could apply to the Special Forces training as well. The Crucible is the final test of a warrior to withstand the conditions and circumstances he or she will face in the normal course of their military life.

A crucible is an instrument or container made from a substance that can withstand great heat and is used for melting or fusing metals or ores. It is, in fact, that hollow at the bottom of a steel furnace where the molten metal collects. That's a metaphor for describing an extreme or severe test in the most adverse circumstances and environment. The extreme test is life itself, the journey to which we all aspire to travel with as much purpose, passion, and peace as possible.

The metals and ores deposited into the crucible of life are the circumstances of rapid change, epitomizing our environment of today. Change is rapid, chaotic, and accelerating at an increasing pace. It overwhelms us with a range of emotions from fear to anxiety, depression, joy, and exultation. We often feel confused and insecure about what is going on, as if we were buffeted about on a stormy sea with little control over our ultimate destination or fate. It seems the greater the change the more resistant we try to become. And, as Anne Morrow Lindberg said, "There is no sin that is punished more implacably by nature than the sin of resistance to change."

CHAOS IN ACTION

An example is what happened after the 9/11 bombing of the World Trade Center twin towers and the Pentagon. One day we were debating how to spend budget surpluses, at peace with the world, and the next day we were in a state of war and back into budget deficits. Enron, a prominent corporate darling went into bankruptcy, an essentially worthless state, after having lost $60 billion in equity in less than six months. The Enron auditor, the proud and premier accounting firm Andersen, was brought to its knees over the Enron debacle. The one constant, it seems, is that change is a fact of life: relentless, rapid, and ruthless.

Contemporary culture is in the grip of a passion to possess and control things. In fact, we are bombarded from all sides with the notion that "having more of something makes us better." It is difficult to prevent being defined as a person by what we have and what others think and say about us. This lust for "things," driven by media of all sorts, has completely lost touch with reality. The continued defining of who we are from external factors accentuates our feelings of being fractured and hurried. I once heard a quote by Henry Ford, who, when asked what it takes to be satisfied, answered, "Just a little bit more." Don't we all sometimes feel this way?

"What is happening?" we ask ourselves. We feel powerless. We lament, blame, and make excuses about the impotence we feel in our circumstances. Nothing new is going on, only more of the same happening at a faster pace. Change, rapid and accelerating, is a fact of life and one that will either be seen by survivors as an opportunity or seen by victims as negative and debilitating.

Niccolo Machiavelli was a 16th century Italian statesman and philosopher who said, "The leader who is not preparing for the next war is a fool. Human nature never changes, only circumstances in which they find themselves. We should, therefore, always live in awareness that things will be in a state of flux and be able to take advantage of it as it happens."

WHAT DO WE DO?

I believe the principles of surviving and thriving in this environment are exactly the same as those one would expect to find in encounters with the physical world. In other words, the same characteristics that work for us in surviving a bear or shark attack, an avalanche, or being lost in the wilderness are exactly the same as those that work in our everyday world of personal, family, and organizational struggles.

THE SECRET TO SURVIVING AND THRIVING

The secret to surviving and thriving is in the recognition of and living the following principle: Life is not about the circumstances we face. These are, for the most part, beyond our span of control. Life is about how we choose to respond to the circumstances we face, and our response is always within our control. This precept is what this book is all about and, in fact, what life is all about. How we choose to respond to the circumstances of life is what either keeps us on the right path to our destination or diverts us into wandering aimlessly and without purpose. This universal precept applies to us as individuals, families, organizations, teams, communities, and nations.

THE KEY TO SURVIVING AND THRIVING

If we had the opportunity to be trained in any of the aforementioned Special Forces or could be given survival training in other military or civilian mountaineering schools, we would learn one overriding, fundamental principle. **Eighty percent of survival is determined by mental attitude, the will to live and not die. Ten percent of survival is based upon having the right resources, and another ten percent is being able to use those resources.** Eighty percent of survival is mental attitude, ten percent is resources, and ten percent is the skill to use those resources.

Remember the movie, *The Edge*, in which Anthony Hopkins and Alec Baldwin portray two lost and hopeless men who have crashed in a small plane in Alaska without resources? As Baldwin's character was coming apart emotionally and on the verge of giving up, Hopkins' character calmly asked the question, "Do you know why people die in the wilderness?" Hopkins answered his own question and said the words that summed up the entire experience: "They die of shame. They beat themselves up, they feel sorry for themselves, wallow in their own self pity, and then they die." Baldwin asks the antidote for this, and Hopkins' response is, "They think."

This exchange frames the proposition and gives us a clear picture of two choices. Do we allow circumstances to control us or do we control ourselves? The answer to this question is fundamental to whether we survive and thrive or wither and die, not just physically but emotionally, mentally, and spiritually.

Within the wilderness of the human mind and spirit, survival is the ultimate choice. Some choose not to live and others choose to live and never give up. These choices are not new; they have been with us since the beginning of time and are only hidden beneath the facade of a modern world. Wilderness can take a person back a thousand generations. Alone at night, away from the lights, sounds, and roads, we are returned to a primal world. Quickly our confidence in "normal" secure surroundings fades, and there are moments when we are overwhelmed with a wave of fear.

We long for a fire. The warmth, comfort, and security become vital for us. The shadows are suddenly unfamiliar and hold the outlines of lions, tigers, and bears waiting to pounce. If we allow it, our emotions are carried away, and we are paralyzed with the fear of what might happen to us. This craving for familiar and comfortable surroundings reflects our deepest need for security and significance.

Have you ever experienced this kind of fear? I don't mean the fear of lions, tigers, and bears but the fear of change, the fear of failure, the fear of not measuring up, the fear of being rejected or isolated. Ever been paralyzed by these emotions, unable to act and make good choices? I guess we all have at some point in our lives. The question is not whether we experience fear but rather what we choose to do about it. What can we do to determine what our attitude will be when we find ourselves in this situation? I propose that this kind of psychological fear, or fear of the future, is the most debilitating emotion we have and one that will prevent us from surviving and thriving if we allow it.

FEAR DEBILITATES US!

A series of difficulties arrives when we are debilitated by psychological fear. Accidents are more likely to happen, we tend to blame others, make excuses, and simply do not process and think very well. As change and ambiguity escalates, we have less self-confidence and become even more debilitated, thus making even poorer choices.

It is easy and natural for us to say that our surroundings are against us. In fact, our surroundings and difficulties are there to aid us, and all those outward circumstances over which we lose our peace of mind are the very conditions necessary to our development. It is only by meeting and overcoming them that we can learn and grow.

Words and their meanings are important. Therefore it is fundamental that we agree on the meaning of the word **attitude**, as we will be using it many times. Many people believe that attitude is determined by circumstances. The proposition of this book is that attitude is not determined by circumstances but rather **REVEALED BY CIRCUMSTANCES**.

If this is true, then our ability to change and process ambiguity, confusion, etc. has been determined before the circumstances reveal themselves. We have predetermined that we will react either negatively or positively, to live or choose to die, to think or to come apart. Why, then, do we spend so much time trying to accumulate the right resources and the skills to use them when eighty percent of surviving and thriving is mental attitude?

Attitude training and changing the way we think are far more important than resources and skills. Daniel Goleman, in his book Emotional Intelligence, promoted the idea of an Emotional Quotient measurement being equally as important as an Intelligence Quotient, or IQ. Emotional intelligence is simply choosing our attitude and responses as opposed to being controlled by them.

ATTITUDE IS EVERYTHING

Author Carolyn Warner said, "I am convinced that attitude is the key to success or failure in almost all of life's endeavors. Your attitude, your perspective, your outlook determines your priorities, actions, and values. Your attitude determines how you interact with yourself and others."

Chuck Swindoll said, "Attitude, to me, is more important than facts. It is more important than the past, education, money, circumstances, failures, success, or what other people think or say or do. It is more important than appearance, giftedness, or skill. It will make or break an organization, family, or a person. The remarkable thing is, we have a choice every day regarding the attitude we embrace for the day. We cannot change the fact that people will act in a certain way. We cannot change the inevitable. The only thing we can do is act on the one string we have, and that is our attitude. I am convinced that life is ten percent what happens to me and ninety percent how I react to what happens to me."

Viktor Frankl was a psychiatrist and the author of Man's Search For Meaning. Frankl, imprisoned in a concentration camp by the Nazis during World War II, suffered incredible mistreatment. This is what he said: "God chooses what we go through. We choose how we go through it. The one feeling you cannot take away from me is the way I choose to respond to what you do to me. The last of one's freedoms is to choose one's attitude in any given circumstance."

General Colin Powell, in his book My American Journey, wrote, "I decided a long time ago that if I had to play on the short end of the field because of discrimination or any other reason, then I would be the best player on that end."

In his book Mere Christianity, C.S. Lewis wrote, "Every time you make a choice you are turning the control part of you, the part that chooses, into something a little different from what it was before. And taking your life as a whole, with all your innumerable choices, you are slowly turning this control thing into a heavenly creature or into a hellish one."

All five people testify to the same basic precept, that life is uncertain, difficult, and inherently unfair. So what? The only question we have to answer is what are we going to do about it. Life is about having the right attitude that determines in advance how we will react to the circumstances with which we are confronted.

I read a *Harvard Business Review* interview with Coach Roberta Fusaro of Boston College that I really liked. It was on the subject of attitude. The men's basketball team at Boston College had enjoyed an amazing turnaround in the 2000-2001 season, rebounding from last place the previous year to first place, with essentially the same starting five players. Fusaro was asked how he explained the turnaround. This is how he responded:

> *When times are bad–and have been bad for several seasons or quarters–it's easy for people to get defensive about who they are and what they can do. They want to blame other people, other teams, and other departments. That's when leaders need to get team members to drop their guard and respond when they are told, 'We want you to do things a little differently.' It's tough to do that until you can sweep all the individual agendas off the court, so to speak. In our case, an intense summer trip to Europe isolated the group from families and friends and forced teammates to deal with one another directly and honestly. They had no one to blame–or to lean on–but themselves. They learned to communicate with one another more constructively.*
>
> *That off-site experience also made the guys more aware of the*

sacrifices necessary to move the team to a new level. They start-ed to focus on using their talents to help the team win, not on their lack of playing time. I guess the same would happen in business: Team members should selflessly match the right skills to the right tasks at the right times.

The only changes we made from the losing season to the winning one were mental changes; the offensive and defensive strategies were essentially the same, as were the workout routines. The things that upset me or drew praise from me stayed the same from season to season–it wasn't about the results. You have to focus on the process of turning things around; if you pay too much attention to wins and losses, you'll always be disappointed.

SURVIVAL IS A CHOICE

How do we choose to survive? What is the secret of a Special Forces commando lost or trapped behind enemy battle lines? First, a decision to live must be made. Once that choice is determined, surviving is natural. Without this decision to live, and not die, survival is impossible. A will to live and thrive is simply a decision that some things are unfinished, including life.

Yet the choice is easy not to make. When circumstances are difficult and seem insurmountable, it is often easier to give up or leave the problems of survival to others. If we are unhappy or depressed, a passive resignation can set in, we feel sorry for ourselves, make excuses, and blame others. Left unchecked, this is the beginning of the end, living in a self-created prison cell. We become whatever we think, and if we think we are powerless and a helpless victim, that is what, with absolute certainty, will surely happen.

I like the following E.J. Hardy story, which illustrates the point: "How dismal you look!" said a bucket to his companion, as they were going to the well. "Ah!" replied the other, "I was reflecting on the uselessness of our being filled, for, let us go away ever so full, we always come back empty." "Dear me! How strange to look at it that way," said the other bucket; "now, I enjoy the thought that however empty we come, we always go away full. Only look on it in that light, and you will be as cheerful as I am."

Attitude is the most important element of surviving and thriving. With the proper attitude, almost anything is possible. One of my favorite stories is of Hugh Glass, the 19th century trapper of Western legend. Glass was horribly mauled by a grizzly bear while deep in hostile Indian territory and left for dead by his two companions. One of his companions was a man by the name of Jim Bridger, who would later become one of the most famous men of the American West. Left for dead, his rifle taken by his companions, and unable to walk, Glass literally crawled to a trading post some two hundred miles away, halfway across the present state of South Dakota. He later forgave his companions for leaving him. When asked how he survived he said, "I made a decision not to die. I refused to die, life had more for me and I wasn't going to let my situation defeat me."

What type of attitude promotes surviving and thriving? Case studies of survivors illustrate certain human qualities are present: Many are stubborn, and although they may be quiet and flexible in their views, an underlying strength prevails. They are persevering, dogmatic, and determined about living. In an uncomfortable environment, they set out to control what they can and avoid trying to control what they cannot. While they may become aggressive toward their plight, they do not become aggressive toward others.

Some people blame themselves and others for getting lost, for making a decision that led to the crisis. In turn, they drive themselves unreasonably, punish themselves, and even turn their aggression on others. When this happens, energy that should be pointed toward solving the problem is channeled into making the crisis worse.

WHAT SHOULD MY ATTITUDE BE?

What should I have decided **before** venturing into a wilderness experience in bear country or traversing the even more difficult journey of life?

- I will survive and thrive!

- I will be prepared by learning about bear behavior and how I should respond!

- I will have a situational awareness of my surroundings!

- I will carry whatever resources help me!

- I will continually learn and seek additional information!

- I will realistically assess my capabilities before I put myself in any situation!

- I will respond with reasoned decisions!

- I will refuse to give up!

- I will focus on controlling what I can control and release what I cannot control!

- I will accept fear as a normal reaction, but I will not allow it to control me!

One of the greatest stories I have heard regarding surviving and thriving is that of Charlie Plumb. We use his experience and personal testimony in our training at Team Trek. Charlie was an F-4 Phantom jet fighter pilot shot down over North Vietnam in the mid 1960s who spent six years as a prisoner of war with two hundred other pilots in the Hanoi Hilton. After graduation from the U.S. Naval Academy, Charlie was sent to Pensacola, Florida, for naval flight training. He then moved on to San Diego where he received further training before being shipped off on the aircraft carrier *Kitty Hawk* for combat service in Vietnam. During the process, he married his high school sweetheart from his hometown in Kansas.

After seventy-five combat missions over North Vietnam, Charlie was downed by an enemy surface-to–air missile. He was captured, tortured for military information, and imprisoned. Charlie calls these years in the "University of Hanoi" a priceless education and the most valuable six years of his life. How can this be? It sounds absurd to us on the outside looking in that a person would be capable of surviving and thriving in this kind of environment. What happened?

Charlie says in his testimony that his education at the "University of Hanoi" began with finding himself in an eight-foot-by-eight-foot cell, not only cut off from the outside world but from his fellow American prisoners too. It was here that he had to make the critical decision of living or dying. He shares candidly that his initial emotion was one of intense fear of what was going to happen to him. Following on this fear were feelings of shame, anger, and bitterness toward those he deemed responsible for his plight. He began to wallow in self-pity, blame others, make excuses, and whine; his country was at fault, his president, U.S. Congress, the builders and mechanics of the plane, virtually everyone except HIMSELF.

The first American contact Charlie had was with Lt. Commander Bob Shoemaker, who occupied the prison cell next to him. Shoemaker initiated the contact by extending a wire through a hole at the base of the cell wall and scratching on the concrete floor in code. Charlie had two reactions to this wire: First, he knew it probably came from an American on the other side of the wall; second, he was afraid to pull on it. Why? Because he was afraid that the person on the other side of the wall might see him the way he saw himself. Ever experienced that kind of fear? I know I have.

After finally getting the courage to tug on the wire and to begin communicating with Shoemaker, Charlie used the opportunity to vent his anger, bitterness, and self-pity. Shoemaker listened to Charlie and then queried him with this: "Do you want to know your biggest problem?" Shoemaker asked. "You mean I have problems bigger than the ones I can see?" Charlie answered. Shoemaker then diagnosed Charlie with what he termed "prison thinking, and it can kill you if you let it."

"Tell me more about prison thinking," Charlie said. Shoemaker responded, "Well, when you get shot down, the normal red-blooded American thing to do is to blame others and to make excuses. The first thing you know, your energy is totally absorbed in feeling sorry for yourself and you are hopelessly enmeshed in prison thinking."

"What is the antidote for prison thinking?" Charlie asked. Shoemaker then proceeded to tell Charlie the antidote was having **an attitude of faith, commitment, and pride,** and Charlie testifies that these three things were more important to his survival than the rice he ate or the water he drank.

It was this counsel from Shoemaker that helped Charlie recover from thinking of himself as a prisoner. Not the concrete-and-steel kind but those prisons of mind and spirit that prevent us from healthy risk and becoming all that we can.   Charlie rediscovered this when he was released from prison after six years and returned home. Upon returning, he was told that his wife had not waited for him and in fact had filed for divorce and was engaged to another man. This was yet another choice for him on life's journey: should he be angry and bitter toward his wife or take responsibility for himself, pick up the pieces of his life and move on? He chose to stay out of that mental prison and instead moved on with his life, remarrying and enjoying a successful career as a public speaker, sharing with others what he has learned about himself.

Prison thinking is a belief that we are powerless to exercise control over how we respond to our circumstances. It is also known as "victim thinking" or "stinking thinking" and directs us to see ourselves as pitiable, whining little bundles of human flesh buffeted to and fro by an environment over which we have no control. This kind of thinking is endemic in our society today, and most of us spend our time making excuses and blaming others for why we cannot do something. Prison thinking is the most debilitating factor we face as individuals, teams, organizations, communities, and as a nation. George Bernard Shaw captured it best when he said, "This is the true joy in life, being used for a purpose recognized as a mighty one ... the being a force of nature instead of a feverish, selfish little clod of ailments and grievances, complaining that the world will not devote itself to making you happy."

Positive mental attitude determines we will take responsibility for what we can control and release what we cannot control. Survivors do not waste energy making excuses and casting blame on others. They will their bodies and minds to survive and not to die, thereby seeing everything as an opportunity. They thrive in the process.

We reside in the crucible of life whether we realize it or not; we have no choice about this. The crucible is what gathers the molten ores and metals of the circumstances, experiences, and beliefs of our lives. It distills and purifies through intense heat and stress, breaking down the molecules to produce something tested, stronger, better, and more usable. Swindoll was right when he said that life is ten percent what happens to us and ninety percent how we respond to what happens to us. We are in fact whatever we think and choose to become. Georgia Douglas Johnson reflected it well in the following poem:

> *Your world is as big as you make it,*
> *I know, for I used to abide*
> *In the narrowest nest in a corner,*
> *My wings pressing close to my side.*
>
> *I battered the cordons around me*
> *And cradled my wings on the breeze,*
> *Then soared to the uttermost reaches*
> *With rapture, with power, with ease.*

THE CRUCIBLE - KEY POINTS

- Life is difficult and uncertain.

- Change is relentless, rapid, and ruthless.
- Fear of the future debilitates us.

- Attitude is not determined by circumstances but rather revealed by them.

- Surviving and thriving is a choice.

- Our nature is to make excuses, rationalize, and blame others.

- Prison thinking is believing we are powerless to change our circumstances.

- We live in a crucible of life whose function is to purify and make us stronger.

- The leader who is not preparing for the next war is a fool.

KEY PRINCIPLES

- Adversity and difficulty make us stronger by giving us greater powers of opposition. Success is not measured by what a person has accomplished; rather by the difficulties they have encountered and the courage with which they overcame them.

- Life is not about the circumstances we face. These are, for the most part, beyond our control. Life is about how we choose to respond to the circumstances we face, and our response is always within our control.

- The key to survival is attitude. Our ability to survive and thrive is eighty percent attitude, ten percent resources, and ten percent knowing how to use those resources.

KEY QUESTIONS

- The German philosopher Friedrich Nietzsche said, "What does not kill me makes me stronger." Do you agree with this statement? Why or why not?

- Can you think of a time when psychological fear, or fear of the future, of failing, kept you from doing the right thing?

- Charlie Plumb, reflecting on his time in a North Vietnamese prison cell, said, "I was afraid to tug on the wire, even though I knew an American was on the other end, because I didn't want him to see me the way I saw myself." Have you ever felt this way? When and why?

THINKING

---

*You can never tell what your thoughts will do,
in bringing you hate or love, for thoughts are
things, and their airy wings are swift as a
carrier dove. They follow the law of the
universe—each thing must create its kind—
and they speed o'er the track to bring you
back, whatever went out from your mind.*

- Ella Wheeler Wilcox

The reason change is difficult for us is that it makes us feel insecure and challenges our core beliefs. If we are not firmly grounded in what we believe we are buffeted to and fro like a leaf in the wind, rising and falling depending upon its direction and speed.

We may say we want change, but the fact is we only want change that is predictable and known to us. Most change does not fall into this category, thus we stay in situations we are familiar with, even if destructive, because we are afraid of changing. "My situation may be crummy but at least it's a secure crummy," we subconsciously think and act out.

Most people do not change until the pain of not changing is greater than the pain of changing. Let me repeat: MOST PEOPLE DO NOT CHANGE UNTIL THE PAIN OF NOT CHANGING IS GREATER THAN THE PAIN OF CHANGING. This means that we do not change until we are so unhappy with our current situation that we make a decision to do something about it. Change implies that we change the way we think about our current circumstances and we cause some different result through our actions.

WHAT NEEDS TO HAPPEN?

For this to occur, something fundamental must transpire. We must see ourselves as the PROBLEM AND THE SOLUTION and believe we have the power to effect a positive response to the situation. This brings us back to attitude. We must change the way we think about change and our ability to respond to it. If we believe change is negative, then that will frame our response; if we view change as positive that also will frame our response.

They must often change, who would be constant in happiness and wisdom.

- Confucius

FREE WILL AND CHOICE

Human beings are endowed with a free will, the will to choose our actions and reactions to life. We are free to choose freedom or restriction, joy or misery, according to the most cherished beliefs and attitudes we hold. If this is true, then we are also free to override those self-limiting, negative beliefs that might even contribute to our circumstances by attracting to ourselves those things we think or believe.

Free will brings with it an awesome responsibility and implies that we always have the ability to recreate our lives by making different choices. The first step in recreating our lives is to have an attitude that we can do it.

Changing results, like the Phoenix, rises from the dead ashes of recognizing the real problem. It is not circumstances, heredity, environment, or anything else that constrains us. It is we ourselves. We are the problem and the solution and when we alter what we believe about change, we will change how we act toward change.

This is what Shoemaker called "prison thinking" when he told Plumb the antidote for his disease. "When we think we are a prisoner, we are a prisoner, not of our physical environment but those prisons of the mind, emotion, and spirit."

A person who can see change as positive, regardless of the situation, and who takes responsibility for his or her reactions is more likely to create great things of lasting value and impact. People who aspire to be great are in control of their own responses and inspire others to be great.

Personal mastery involves taking responsibility for changing the way we think and transforming the belief system that dictates our responses to change and circumstances. When we believe that the cause of our lack of peace and joy is a result of others, then we will never pass beyond it. But when we perceive the cause of the problem is in the way we think, then we have taken the first step toward solving that problem and the peace and joy that come with it. Enlightened and empowered people have given up the delusion that others are the cause of our misery. We have grasped the profound truth that circumstances have only revealed the real cause, which is the way in which we respond to those circumstances.

People who apply their energy to making excuses, blaming, complaining, and whining have given themselves over to a sure prison cell. They have given up control of themselves and instead have bound themselves over to whatever person or situation controls their thoughts and actions. The fool meets anger with anger, strife with strife, always tit for tat. The person who has mastery over self instead applies energy to meeting anger with peace, hatred with love, negative with positive, and returns good for evil.

UNIVERSAL PRINCIPLES

The transformed life is ruled by truth and principles. Purpose and core values are consistent with these principles and the actions of our lives are played out in concert and balance. The way we think and view the world is driven by these universal principles and purpose rather than our pitiable, self-centered efforts to protect ourselves. Though we may be physically constrained, as Plumb was, and even if our bodies are racked by pain, we can have peace and joy in our mind and spirit.

What are these principles? One is that peace and turmoil cannot dwell together. To know this is to be prepared to choose between the two, to accept the former and reject the latter. For example, hatred and love cannot dwell in the same heart. Where one abides, the other cannot.

A universal principle of life is that we have choices, and only through choosing one can the other be routed out. We receive what we want by giving up what we don't want.

An example of this is that, in our interactions with others, there is always the battle between control and influence. The governing principle is that the more we try to control others the less influence we actually have with them. It is a great paradox. It doesn't make sense, doesn't fit with what we believe about the world. The more out-of-control we feel, the more we try to control and the less influence we have--the opposite result from what we are seeking.

It is only by giving up trying to control the uncontrollable that we achieve peace, our influence increases, and we are more likely to receive what we desire. This is a great paradox of life. We are what we think, and what we think determines our choices, and what we choose determines our course in life. If we want to change the way we respond to circumstances of life then we must first change the way we think.

> *If you teach a man to keep his eyes upon what others think of him, unthinkingly to live the life and hold the ideas of the majority of his contemporaries, you must discredit in his eyes the authoritative voice of his own soul. He may be a docile citizen; he will never be a man. It is our choice, on the other hand, to disregard this babble and chattering of other men better and worse than we are, and to walk straight before us what light we have. It is by truth and principle that we must live and stand or fall.*
>
> - Robert Louis Stevenson

REALITY VERSUS ILLUSION

A fundamental mismatch between the reality of a problem and how we think about that problem frequently exists. This is the enemy of productive change in individuals and organizations and occurs when we focus on the symptoms rather than the problem itself. We are either in denial that issues exist or go for short-term relief that only masks the problem rather than solving it.

As we tend to blame others and outside influences for our problems, we later find there are not any outside influences to blame; it is the way in which we think about the problem. Solving problems and dealing with change always begin from within, and the cure lies in our relationship with the "enemy." And, as the cartoon character Pogo said, "I have met the enemy and he is me." Change the way we think about the system in which we live, and we will change the way we act within that system. This all begins with an attitude of seeing ourselves as the problem and the solution.

SEEING OURSELVES WITH CLARITY

A strategy is trying to understand where you sit in today's world. Not where you wish you were or where you hoped you would be, but where you are. It's trying to understand where you want to be five years out. It's assessing the realistic chances of getting from here to there.

- Jack Welch

Plato told us 2,500 years ago that "the unexamined life is not worth the living." Jack Welch, former CEO of General Electric Corporation, tells us the same thing today. We must continually examine ourselves with all the clarity and courage we possess. To do otherwise is to live a life without purpose and direction, not really living at all but simply existing in a self-formed prison cell, blaming others and making excuses for why we cannot take control of our own lives.

In order to change the way we think, we must cease to dwell on the pessimistic and commence to live free from the constraints of prison thinking. If we want to influence others to be positive, we must be positive; if we would have others free from wrong thinking; we must be free. We can transform and influence everything around us if we first transform ourselves.

As part of Plumb's testimony, he spoke of something his coach told him that he never forgot. Coach Smith told him, "Whether you think you are a winner or a loser, you are right."

"Coach, I don't know what that means," Plumb responded.

"I don't want you coming back here in ten years and telling me the reason you failed is because you went to this little bitty high school. I don't want you coming back here in fifteen years and telling me the reason your marriage failed is because your wife turned off bad, because the difference in success or failure is you," Coach Smith said.

What we think reflects what we choose, and choices initiate action. Actions have consequences either positive or negative. This poem by Anna Russell illustrates the process of faulty thinking:

I went to see my psychiatrist to be psychoanalyzed.

To find out why I killed my cat and
blackened my wife's eyes.

He put me on a downy couch to see what he could find.
And this is what he dredged up from my subconscious mind.

When I was one my mommy hid my
dolly in the trunk.

And so it follows naturally that
I am always drunk.

When I was two I saw my father
kiss the maid one day.

And that's why I suffer now
from Kleptomania.

When I was three I suffered ambivalence
from my brothers,

And so it follows naturally,
that I poisoned all my lovers.

I'm so glad I have learned the
lesson it has taught.

That everything I do is someone else's fault.

To achieve personal mastery we must first see the enemy, and the enemy is ourselves. To conquer and be victorious, worthless chaos-producing elements must be eradicated from our mind. These elements consist of bitterness, hatred, jealousy, pride, self-seeking vanity, and delusion. The transformation of the mind would replace the ignoble elements with virtuous characteristics: patience, love, humility, self-reliance, wisdom, empathy, and compassion.

WHAT HINDERS US?

What hinders us in the quest for personal mastery? **Fear hinders us**: Fear of seeing ourselves the way we really are, fear of failure, perfectionism, rejection, and vulnerability. Fear causes us to build walls to change, delude ourselves, and perpetuate false beliefs. Remember we do not seek real change until the pain of not changing is greater than the pain of changing.

William Shakespeare's phrase, "To thine own self be true," becomes the basis for personal change. We must have the courage and integrity to lead that person we see in the mirror each morning. And having come to the point where we realize we are absolutely responsible for our every action we will have come a long way on the journey to peace, purpose, and passion. If we are to rise, let us choose to cease thinking the weak and foolish thought that "others hinder us," and let us set out to discover that we only hinder ourselves.

I close the chapter on thinking with a quote I like very much from James Allen:

> *A man's mind may be likened to a garden, which may be intelligently cultivated or allowed to run wild; but whether cultivated or neglected, it must, and will, bring forth. If no useful seeds are put into it, then an abundance of useless weed seeds will fall into it, and will continue to produce their worthless kind.*

THINKING - KEY POINTS

- We are what we think.

- We are the problem and the solution.

- Change should be viewed as positive and an opportunity to grow.

- We have a free will and the ability to choose our reactions.

- If we give over control of our responses to circumstances we are a prisoner of those circumstances.

- The transformed life is ruled by truth and principles.

- There is a mismatch between the reality of a problem and our perception of it.

- We must continually examine ourselves with clarity and courage.

KEY PRINCIPLES

- To change the way in which we respond to the circumstances of life, we must first change the way we think. What we think determines our choices, and our choices determine our course in life. We are a compilation of all our choices.

- It is only by giving up trying to control the uncontrollable that we can attain peace, our influence increases, and we can achieve what we desire. This is one of the great paradoxes of life.

- A person's mind is like a garden, which may be cultivated or allowed to run wild. Whichever is allowed, the mind will bring forth something either for good or not. We will reap that which we sow in our mind, later than we sow, and more than we sow.

KEY QUESTIONS

- Coach Smith said to Charlie Plumb, "If you think you are a winner or a loser, you are right." What did he mean by this?

- Can you think of an example of "prison thinking" in your life? Is there anyone against whom you harbor anger, resentment, or bitterness?

- What are you sowing in your mind? What books are you reading? Movies? Television programs? Do you agree that you are what you put in your mind?

NAVIGATING CHANGE

*The main concern of a person is not to find
pleasure or avoid pain but to find meaning
and purpose in life.*

- Oswald Chambers

One of the basic tenets of life is that change exists: accelerating, relentless, liberating, sometimes unfair, and ruthless. We have very little control over our circumstances, but we have total control over how we respond to those circumstances. In fact, control over our own reactions is really the only control we do have. How do we do this? How do we navigate the valleys, mountains, and rivers of life while enveloped under a forest canopy that sometimes prevents us from even seeing the sky?

A fundamental fact of life is we are on a journey to somewhere. Our life begins and our life ends, and in between is what we leave behind as a legacy to our families, friends, and organizations of which we are a part. This legacy is all we will leave behind and the question we must think about is this: How will people remember us, what impact have we made on their lives, what good have we wrought during our stay on this earth?

I like the quote by Henry Ward Beecher, who said, "We should so live and labor in our time that what comes to us as seed may go to the next generation as fruit." He is speaking of the law of the harvest. Whatever is sown will be harvested, later than it is sown, and more than is sown. We must then purpose to sow that which we want to harvest. Whatever we think in our minds and hearts is what we are and what we will become. To think otherwise is insanity.

MY MAP

I am a person who thinks in visual pictures. If I can envision a concept or idea, then it is easier for me to understand its implications. As I see myself on this journey of life, navigating through all the pitfalls of changing circumstances that inevitably confront me, I like to think of myself as a map. And the map I see is a topographical map.

A topographical map is an extremely valuable tool. It is made from an aerial photograph of a specified area and reveals, via symbols, everything that the camera itself saw. What the camera saw were rivers, creeks, ponds, lakes, roads, trails, forest, clearings, power lines, buildings, and terrain contour lines. This map and its contents are invaluable when navigating through and about the area.

There is, however, a fundamental problem. For the map to have value, it must be oriented in the correct direction by a compass. As the map is lying flat on a surface, the top is always north, bottom south, right side east, and left side west. Thus the map must be turned so the top is always pointed or oriented to the north. To have the top of the map pointed south would cause us to be looking in the wrong direction. To navigate successfully through difficult terrain, both a topographical map and a compass are required

The map represents such things as my personality type, my temperament, and my intellectual and physical capabilities. Certainly it would include my life experiences, skills, and abilities as well. These things are of value and contribute to my journey through life. They are, however, of much lower value if they are not oriented correctly. Orienting my map and compass is what keeps me on the right course.

MY COMPASS

If the map is a picture of myself, then what does the compass represent? The compass is something outside myself, providing direction and consisting of three components.

- Core Values

- Core Purpose

- Vision

First, core values. Core values are non-negotiable, unchanging tenets stating what is of utmost importance to me. They are basic to how I live and conduct my life. Examples are such things as integrity, continual growth, love, family, and allegiance to country. Values vary by individual and are subjective.

Second, core purpose. Core purpose answers the question about why I exist. What am I doing on this earth and what is my purpose for being here?

Third, future desired state or vision. What do I want to become? What do I want to look like in five years, not just physically but emotionally, intellectually, and spiritually? For me to travel to the destination I want to reach, I must have a set of core values, a core purpose, and I certainly need to know what I want to look like when I get there.

I like to tell a story from *Alice In Wonderland* which I will paraphrase: Alice is wandering through Wonderland, and she comes upon a fork in the road. Sitting in the middle of the fork is the Cheshire cat. Alice asks the cat which road she should take, and the cat answers, "Where do you want to go?" "I don't know," Alice answers, and the cat responds, "Then either road will do."

This illustrates the insanity of wandering through life without a personal compass. If we don't know who we are, our purpose and destination, then we will get somewhere, we just don't know where. Remember the definition of insanity: doing the same thing over and over again but expecting different results.

We all wander and get off course. This is basic to the human condition and is a part of our map. What keeps us on course is our personal compass, a tool we can use in conjunction with our map. Our map may deceive us, but our compass never lies. The red tip of the magnetic needle always points north, giving us consistent and unchanging direction to our life. The map and compass in combination with each other make an unbeatable tool! Navigating Change consists of following certain precepts representing truth and laws. Follow the precepts, and navigation will be easy, violate the precepts and the consequences will be equally sure.

THE SEVEN PRECEPTS OF NAVIGATING CHANGE

1. POSITIVE EXPECTATION
- 100% Responsibility
- Opportunity exists in all circumstances

2. KNOW YOUR CURRENT LOCATION
- Self examination
- Commitment to truth

3. DETERMINE YOUR DESTINATION
- Create a personal compass
- Envision a desired end state

4. ORIENT YOUR MAP AND COMPASS
- Align who you are with where you want to go
- Live with personal integrity

5. DEVELOP AN INCREMENTAL PLAN
- Create an action plan for reaching your destination
- Determine actionable items

6. COLLECT FEATURES AS YOU GO
- Daily quiet time of self examination
- Seek feedback and accountability

7. HAVE A STOPPING POINT
- Admit when you are off course
- Make amends if necessary
- Rework the process

NAVIGATING CHANGE ENABLES US TO DEAL WITH PARADOX

Navigating Change is about attaining the attitude and the skills to successfully navigate whatever twist and turn life may give us. There are two great paradoxes in this journey through life:

- The more certain of the details of the future, the greater the likelihood we are wrong.

- Whatever we expect the future to be, we must anticipate it won't be.

We are living in a time in which change is occurring at such a rate that it seems we are in a permanent paradox. Synergy is the shifting of opposites where two different and opposing forces combine to produce something greater than either could produce independently. The speed at which this is happening is simply dizzying. It is here that the law of unintended consequences abounds. I can remember not many years ago when AT&T was a superpower alone atop the telecommunications industry. Today, they are a follower about to be swallowed by companies that ten years ago we had barely heard of. Think of the demise of the Soviet Union following the fall of the Berlin Wall. Who could have anticipated these things?

What is next? We don't know! What we do know is that it will be rapid, relentless, and ruthless. We must focus on the one thing we can control, and this is our attitude toward this change. A few years ago, I wrote the following poem, which illustrates the point:

SELF-LEADERSHIP

I am my own raw material.
Only when I know of what I am made,
where I want to go,
And my purpose, can I begin to live my life.
Otherwise I am fastened to circumstances and
Constrained by the opinions of others.
Only when I see my own possibilities,
Ability to influence and serve others in a positive way,
Am I able to move forward, achieving,
Excellence and balance in my life.
The fruit of this realization will be manifested
In my relationship with God
and fellow human beings.

NAVIGATING CHANGE - KEY POINTS

• Life is a journey.

• Our legacy will be the impact we have had on the lives of
others.

• A topographical map is a metaphor representing our skills,
abilities, intellect, personality, and experiences.

• A compass is a metaphor representing our core purpose,
core values, and vision.

• Orienting or aligning our map and compass is what keeps us
on course.

• Our nature is to wander off course.

• Following certain precepts of navigation is what keeps us
on course.

KEY PRINCIPLES

• Navigating through the forests and valleys of life requires a
personal compass to align and orient us in the correct
direction. This compass consists of our purpose, values,
and vision.

- Navigating Change consists of following certain precepts. Follow the seven precepts and navigation will be easy, violate the precepts and the consequences will be sure.

- Change is occurring so rapidly that it seems we are in a permanent paradox where the shifting of opposites is constant It is here the law of unintended consequences abounds.

KEY QUESTIONS

- Oswald Chambers said, "The main concern of a person is not to find pleasure or avoid pain but to find meaning and purpose in life." What does he mean?

- Does the picture of Alice wandering through the Wonderland, coming upon forks in the road that require certain choices resonate with you ?

- Can you think of choices you have made in your life that, when viewed in retrospect, turned out to be extremely critical junctures? Did those choices have the consequences you intended or did not intend?

POSITIVE EXPECTATION

*The real voyage of discovery lies not in seek-
ing new landscapes, but in having new eyes.*

-Marcel Proust
French Philosopher

Positive Expectation is embracing the inevitability of change as both expected and positive. It is the attitude that whatever the circumstances or situation, some good can result. It is also having the attitude of 100% Responsibility toward our ability to respond to and affect the circumstances in some manner.

I can remember sitting and watching as two jumbo jets, loaded with fuel, crashed into the World Trade Center. My response was absolute horror and disbelief and a feeling of being personally violated. Someone had entered my home, America, and killed and maimed for no apparent reason. I am still angry toward those who perpetrated these acts.

I remember discussing this with others and listening to television pundits glumly forecast the "end of the earth" and this being the worst thing that had ever happened to this country. They were right of course about the horror of this but they were also quite wrong about their prediction that no good would come of it.

The truth, of course, is that a succession of attacks had been made on us, from the bombing of our embassy in Africa, to the suicide attack on the U.S. naval vessel Cole. These circumstances or something equally horrible could have been anticipated.

How we view the tragedy has everything to do with what our response is, either negative or positive. Since we can't do anything about the fact that the attacks happened we can choose to view the after affect as positive simply because to do so is the only way we can empower ourselves to do anything about it. What could possibly come out of these circumstances that is positive we may ask?

- We were galvanized as a nation like no other time since Pearl Harbor.

- We assessed our values, how we spend our time, and what is important.

- We returned to our spiritual roots.

- We increased respect for those who defend us, i.e. police, firefighters, CIA, FBI, and certainly our military.

- We tested our political, economic, legal, and social systems and they responded with professionalism and effectiveness.

- We saw the value of family and friends differently.

- Charity abounded. People gave more of their time and money.

- We shifted military priorities, re-engineered our forces, allocating more resources where they were needed.

- Long overdue security measures were instituted at airports and other strategic locations.

Whether we choose to see these as negative or positive depends upon our attitude. Unfortunately, it sometimes takes a horror of this magnitude to transport us back to the basics. The positive aspect is that we did it and many good things were produced as a result. This is an example of the principle that **PEOPLE DO NOT CHANGE UNTIL THE PAIN OF NOT CHANGING IS GREATER THAN THE PAIN OF CHANGING**.

Positive Expectation is about being willing to take a healthy risk with the attitude that something good can come out of it, then processing that experience to determine what learning could result.

PSYCHOLOGICAL FEAR VERSUS REALITY

I heard a saying not long ago that I like: If you are not living on the healthy edge then you are taking up too much room.

Most of us live our lives safely away from the edge, with the gap between where we stand and that edge filled with fear. Psychological fear debilitates us because it deals with the future or what might happen to us. Psychological fear manifests itself in fear of failure, rejection, or looking foolish and prevents us from approaching the edge and becoming all we can be.

By allowing fear to control us, we remain and live our lives in what we at Team Trek call the "comfort zone." In the comfort zone, we feel safe, secure, comfortable, and competent, and things are known and predictable to us. We have walls of defense built up and certain habits and patterns that just feel good to us. To venture outside this zone is to risk the unfamiliar, unknown, uncomfortable, unexpected, unpredictable, and risky. We call this the "new territory," and it is frightening for many of us to think about venturing out into it.

The problem, of course, with living our lives in the "comfort zone" is that we do not grow. We become stale, lose our purpose, and simply drift toward mediocrity or, worse yet, an emotional, spiritual, and intellectual death. We only grow by moving out to the edge of the "comfort zone," where it feels insecure and scary, and taking a big leap with a credible "healthy risk." This is what we call taking a "leap of faith" into the "new territory."

What do we gain? "New territory" becomes "tamed territory," and the comfort zone is suddenly expanded. We have grown, stepped out of the box, enjoyed a success, and expanded our belief in ourselves and whatever it was that we placed our trust and faith in. This stretching of ourselves through a continuous taking of "healthy risk" is what enables us to grow in all areas of our life: physically, spiritually, intellectually, and emotionally.

NO PAIN-NO GAIN

There is a saying in sports that if there is "no pain, there is no gain". We understand this precept very well in the physical world because most of us know what it takes to get ourselves in good physical condition, a lot of pain

No pain, no gain also applies in all other areas of our life. If we are not willing to take "healthy risks" either intellectually in our careers or emotionally with our relationships then the consequence will be no growth. We only grow by stepping out of the box and taking a healthy risk. The following quote from Teddy Roosevelt is one I really like:

> *It is not the critic who counts; not the man who points out how the strong man stumbled or where the doer of deeds could have done them better. The credit belongs to the man who is actually in the arena; whose face is marred by dust and sweat and blood; who strives valiantly; who errs, and comes up short again and again because there is no effort without error and shortcoming; who does actually try to do the deed; who knows the great enthusiasm, the great devotion and spends himself in a worthy cause; who, at worst, if he fails, at least he fails while daring greatly. Far better it is to dare mighty things, to win glorious triumphs even though checkered by failure, than to rank with those poor spirits who neither enjoy nor suffer much because they live in the gray twilight that knows neither victory or defeat.*

What hinders us? Emotions of fear and internal negative self-talk serve to keep us from taking healthy risk. One of the most self-limiting consequences of faulty thinking are the internal conversations we hold with ourselves. Beliefs will surface such as:

- "I can't"

- "I will fail"

- "I am too stupid"

- "I am embarrassed"

- "I will make a fool of myself"

- "I must do it perfectly"

- "It has always been done this way"

- "What will others think of me?"

- "There must be something wrong with me"

When we move to the edge of the comfort zone we not only engage in negative self-talk we can actually feel these feelings in our physical bodies. "I feel paralyzed", or "My heart is going to jump out of my body," are examples. We may experience all this in a few seconds, minutes, or years. Whether we choose to leap into the "new territory" or not will determine our personal growth experience. After taking the leap a person might typically experience the following:

- "I have grown"

- "I have stretched"

- "I kept a promise to myself"

- "I like myself better"

- "I am free"

- "I am ready for the next challenge"

What has happened? We have taken a healthy risk and we have received a big pay off for it. That payoff is our "comfort zone" has been expanded. It has grown by the amount of "new territory" we have taken and has now become "tamed territory". We are ready to move on. But first, we must process what happened, what we have learned, and how we can apply what we have learned.

It is not enough simply to take a "healthy risk"; we must also process the experience. At Team Trek we use a model we call the Experiential Learning Model to show how we learn and how we can process the experience and change behavior. There are four steps:

- Healthy risk -- Did we breach the "comfort zone" constraining line and move into "new territory"?

- What happened? What feelings and emotions did we experience? What were we thinking? What kind of self-talking was going on,negative or positive?

- What does it all mean? What principles were at work, i.e. trust, faith, healthy risk, giving up control, etc. What was the payoff for this experience? How did we feel afterward and what were we telling and feeling about ourselves?

- How do we apply what we have learned either in our personal or professional life?

It is useful and productive to go through this model either with ourselves or with others after we have ventured into "new territory". Processing the experience as soon afterwards as possible is what increases the probability of "new territory" becoming "tamed territory".

The ultimate goal of any experience should be to learn and grow from it. We define learning as not only knowing about something; it is actually converting the knowledge into a change in behavior. When an experience results in changed behavior, then we have learned. If behavior has not changed, we have simply accumulated knowledge about something. Learning means behavior has changed.

A useful tool for processing experiences is a personal journal. A personal journal allows us to record the experience so it is fresh in our mind and our emotions and experiences are still near the surface. It is the time when we are most honest with ourselves about what happened. It also records the experience for us as a history of our learning and growth.

100% RESPONSIBILITY

The second component of Positive Expectation is what we at Team Trek call 100% Responsibility. I believe this principle is foundational to any personal or organizational growth. Without its embodiment in our thinking and actions, we are simply learning about things and not really changing. What is 100% Responsibility?

I am 100% Responsible for how I choose to respond to all circumstances and people in my life. Everyone else is 0% Responsible.

I believe this is the most powerful principle of life because it deals with everything we have discussed in this book thus far. In short it means **NO EXCUSES, NO BLAMING, NO COMPLAINING, AND NO WHINING.** We either did something or we did not and an excuse is not acceptable or exchangeable for desired results.

Remember the example Charlie Plumb used when first talking with Shoemaker. He was looking for someone "to tell his troubles to". Shoemaker listened and then diagnosed Charlie with the disease of "prison thinking". The antidote is 100% Responsibility. We are what we think and subsequently choose. To believe differently violates the Law of the Harvest which dictates that whatever is sown is harvested.

Living our lives with an attitude of 100% Responsibility is not about fairness, in fact, it is inherently **unfair**. There is nothing fair about taking responsibility for reacting to circumstances over which we have no control. 100% Responsibility is about freedom. The freedom to choose and not be controlled by the actions of others or the circumstances we find ourselves in.

How often have you heard someone say; "I am the one who messed up, I take responsibility". On the contrary, there is usually a great deal of posturing with excuses and blame about why this was not our responsibility. The problem with this, of course, is that when we make excuses and blame others we give them control over our life and actions; enormous amounts of time and energy are wasted. We can only think about one thing at a time, thus energy used to make excuses is energy not available to work on the most important issue: how to solve the problem.

At the United States Military Academy at West Point, cadets are introduced to this principle through the manner in which they are required to answer a question or address a problem. Cadets are taught there are only four answers to any question:

- Yes Sir!

- No Sir!

- No excuses Sir!

- I don't understand the question Sir!

On the surface this restriction in communication seems harsh and unfair. After all, shouldn't a person be given the opportunity to give a good reason why they did not accomplish what they were supposed to do? Most of us would believe it is unfair not to be able to give a reason or excuse why something was not accomplished.

What the Academy is trying to teach cadets is to take personal responsibility and ownership of a problem. By accepting responsibility and ownership, energy is devoted to solving the problem rather than finding someone to blame. Thus, the cadet is free to determine and make a reasoned choice about how he or she will respond and is not dependent on or a prisoner to excuses and blame.

Two of the most popular forms of excuses are **BLAMING** others and **JUSTIFYING** lack of results. We are all guilty of this! Think how frequently we hear or say the following kinds of statements:

- "It's not my fault, that's John's job."

- "It's accounting's fault."

- "The reason it failed was operations did not do their part."

- "It's not our responsibility."

Blaming and justifying are ways we can avoid taking responsibility. They have a perfectly rational purpose, that being to avoid punishment, ridicule, or embarrassment, however, as a healthy life strategy they are ineffective and destructive.

If blaming and justifying are such ineffective strategies, why do people use them? I know why I blame or justify. It keeps me from being "wrong" and temporarily helps me save face and not have to look at my behavior. To blame and justify diminishes my personal power and influence. It empowers circumstances instead of me.

A NEW WAY TO THINK: 100% RESPONSIBILITY

I am 100% Responsible for how I choose to respond to all the circumstances and people in my life. Everyone else is 0% Responsible.

I live my life with no excuses, blaming, justifying, or whining! Whatever happens, I did it. Whatever the result, I created it. I am in control of my responses to life's circumstances. I believe this principle is the most powerful and empowering in life and is absolutely foundational to personal and organizational growth. Let's not delude ourselves: if we are not leading the person we see in the mirror each morning, then we are not leading anyone.

Blaming is simply a way of placing responsibility other than on the person doing the blaming. When I blame someone else for what happens, I make others responsible and in control. Blaming keeps me from looking at what I can do to change things.

Justifying is an equally ineffective strategy. We have all heard the following justifications about why results did not turn out as desired:

- "It's really nobody's fault".

- "It could not have been helped".

- "We did the best job we could do".

- "There was nothing else we could do".

Justifying is a subtle way for us to blame someone else for the outcome. Being 100% Responsible means I act as if I alone am responsible even though there are things beyond my control. I do not wait for my boss, colleagues, subordinates, spouse, or anyone else to assume responsibility for creating a result I desire. I am 100% Responsible, period. Acting as if I am 100% Responsible, there is no room for blaming and justifying. There are no excuses, only results.

Living a life of 100% Responsibility involves taking healthy risk, lots of it. The reward for this kind of risk is:

- We are effective human beings.

- We create results we want in our personal and professional life.

- We influence others to follow us.

How do we exercise influence with others as a result of this behavior?

- They appreciate the results.

- They like not being blamed for the lack of results.

• They like not listening to justifications and excuses.

How do we influence ourselves as a result of this behavior?

• Our lives work better.

• We are free.

• We feel better about ourselves.

• We devote our energies to productive solutions.

Imagine the personal empowerment of an individual or organization in which everyone assumes and leads their life with no excuses, where there is actually a rush to assume ownership of a problem. Perhaps the greatest value of this principle is that it focuses energy on creating solutions to problems. It energizes the person and the organization in a way nothing else can. There is nothing more empowering than 100% Responsibility.

In summary and perspective, 100% Responsibility is an effective life strategy, however, it is not perfect, just as I am not perfect. Even though I act as if I am 100% Responsible, there may be times when I cannot produce the results I want because events are beyond my control. Having said that, I still choose to live my life this way because to do otherwise places me in a prison cell of the mind where circumstances control me.

To summarize, positive expectation is personally empowering. It looks for the positive in all circumstances while addressing the reality of our responsibility to effect positive results on those circumstances.

It is living our lives with 100% responsibility that produces freedom. Freedom and responsibility are, in fact, two sides of the same coin. You cannot have one without the other.

POSITIVE EXPECTATIONS - KEY POINTS

- Positive expectation is embracing the inevitability of change as positive.

- Whether we choose to see circumstances as positive or negative is a choice.

- 100% Responsibility is fundamental to navigating change.

- If we are not living on the healthy edge then we are taking too much room.

- Allowing fear to control us keeps us in the "comfort zone".

- It is only through stepping out of the "comfort zone" that we can grow.

- We only grow by stepping out of the box and taking a "healthy risk".

- Processing our experience helps us to learn and change our behavior.

- Excuses and blaming are not a substitute for results.

KEY PRINCIPLES

• I am 100% Responsible for how I choose to respond to the circumstances which confront me in life. Everyone else is 0% Responsible.

• Rationalizing and justifying are ways for us to blame someone else for the outcome. It is a behavior that cripples us because it centers power in someone or something other than ourselves.

• Taking responsibility for our actions and reactions empowers us. It makes our life work better, increases our influence with others and makes us free of the constraints of other people and circumstances.

KEY QUESTIONS

• Ask yourself the question, "If I am not living on the healthy edge then I am taking up too much room." What does this mean?

• Are you living in the "comfort zone", afraid to venture into the "unknown territory"? What hinders you?

• You understand the point "no pain, no gain" in your physical world. How does it apply to your spiritual, intellectual, and emotional life?

KNOW YOUR CURRENT LOCATION

*Seeing and admitting the truth about myself,
about my role in creating my own problems,
and about how I relate to others is vital to my
personal growth and well-being.*

- M. Scott Peck

In navigating through the forest, it is fundamental to know our location before we set out in any direction. If we do not know our location, we should stay in the same general area until we determine where we are. To venture out only leads to more confusion, and it makes any action plan we may have developed worthless or needlessly risky, compounding the problem. Our location is who and where we are.

How do we begin with this self-examination? I believe we are made up of three interdependent components: body, mind, and soul. Using a computer metaphor, the soul represents the software, the mind the hardware or computer, and the body the printer or implementer. I believe the soul is the seat of our belief systems, the mind is the processor of those beliefs, and the body simply carries out the choices that are made.

Should this be true, then our major work must be in our belief systems or paradigms about the way we see the world and our reactions to it. If we do not keep our belief systems cleaned up, they will impact our mind and body. For us to function at maximum capability, all three components must be in concert.

Why do we do virus checks periodically on our computers? Obviously, we do virus checks to rid our computer systems of lies and delusions that would cause it to malfunction in the way it processes information. Unfortunately, most of us don't do our virus checks until we have a problem. Are our mind and soul any different? Whatever we allow to enter our mind is what we will become if it is not eradicated.

Thoughts, beliefs, and attitudes become energized or strengthened when we dwell on them repeatedly and allow them to form a specific and clear intention. The more energy we put into a belief, the deeper imbedded it becomes and the more difficult it is to root out.

We also have the power to energize positive beliefs based on truth in the same manner. The bottom line is we have the free will choice as to what we will believe, dwell upon, and act upon. Beliefs generate thoughts and thoughts generate action, action produces consequences which reinforce beliefs, and we go on and on in a cycle of self-fulfilling prophesy.

This is not to say that all reality is the result of our beliefs. This is simply not true. We must remember that we live in an imperfect world with imperfect human beings. Therefore, many circumstances involving change, chaos, difficulty, etc. simply exist. This brings us back to the importance of attitude, one that accepts the reality that life is difficult and unfair and, as Viktor Frankl, said, "The last of our freedoms is how we choose to react to what someone or something does to us." In its simplest form, this is what life is all about, having a purpose and set of values that we believe in and using them to make reasoned choices about how we react to the circumstances of life.

THE PREREQUISITE TO CHANGE

- An intense desire to change.

- An attitude of 100% Responsibility.

- See myself as the problem and the solution.

- A commitment to truth and honesty.

- A commitment to excellence.

- An attitude of healthy risk.

• An acceptance of the inability to control the uncontrollable.

HUMAN NATURE

In order to understand ourselves, we must first appreciate human nature. I believe that the nature of man is self-serving and defensive, and we suffer from two major delusions:

• We are influenced by evil, outside factors, forcing us to commit ignoble deeds.

• We are essentially good, pure, and seek noble ends.

These two false beliefs form the basis for how we think about the world we live in. The truth is not the evil, outside influences but rather our self-serving view of the world that dwells within us. As long as we are held in bondage to these two false beliefs, we will make excuses, blame others, and make no progress toward our personal growth. To begin personal change and self-mastery, we are required to accept reality; we are the problem, not some external force or factors coercing us to act or behave in certain ways.

Acceptance of the reality of the problem must be followed by a desire to change accompanied by a "teachable spirit." A "teachable spirit" does not mean a person is weak or easily dominated by others. Instead, it denotes strength, in that a person is willing to give up a thought, idea, or belief if it is found to be false and without merit. Being open to the truth comes from an attitude of humility and discernment, of always seeking to grow, learn, and improve.

We must be true to ourselves and possess the moral courage to examine and to change. Socrates said, "The only thing I know absolutely is that I do not know anything." He was saying that his knowledge, relative to the truth available, is miniscule and that, for him to grow and learn, he must be open to accepting new truth and rejecting old false beliefs.

A belief consists of an attitude of mind determining the course of our lives. Belief and action then are inseparable, as the one determines the other. We think, act, and live our lives in exact accordance with our innermost belief system. This is a principle of the Law of the Harvest. We are whatever we believe we are, the mind simply processing this and the body carrying it out in actions.

What do we do and how do we do it? The secret to personal mastery rests on a simple principle. The principle is that we cannot think two things at once. Where one thought abides another cannot. To change, therefore, we must replace the ignoble, non-influencing characteristics with those of noble and virtuous repute. For a transformation of beliefs to occur, we must have clarity about what we do not want to be and what we do want to be. Personal growth involves replacement of the one with the other.

THE LEADER/FOLLOWER MODEL

We have asked hundreds of Team Trek clients participating in our programs the following question: "If you were to describe the characteristics of a person you would follow and give passionately and enthusiastically your head, heart, and hands, what would they look like?" After listening to comments that such a person does not exist, we compile a list. The interesting part of this exercise is that each group determines exactly the same characteristics whether they are a group of corporate executives or an eighth-grade class.

The reason I believe this exercise is useful is that it creates a model for assessing character traits that are admired by us and which influence us to follow. It also creates for us a pool of noble and virtuous traits that we can strive to replace for those other characteristics we seek to rid ourselves of. The results of the model are as follows:

CHARACTERISTICS OF A PERSON
WHO COULD INFLUENCE ME TO FOLLOW WITH
MY HEAD, HEART, AND HANDS

- Good listener
- Has a vision for the organization and for individuals within the organization
- Has clarity of purpose and values
- Positive and enthusiastic
- Encourages, teaches, and mentors
- Acts with 100% Responsibility
- Sense of humor
- Celebrates victories
- Good judgment and common sense
- Able to see the best in people
- Makes others feel valuable and important
- Trustworthy
- Integrity

- Humility

- Patience

- Moral courage

- Open to new ideas

- Selfless and servant attitude

If we examine this list carefully, we discover a common denominator. This person is one who is not personally great but instead is someone who creates a desire in us to be great. In other words, we feel important, needed, and valuable around this person and, as Jack Nicholson said in the movie *As Good As It Gets*, "You make me want to be a better person." Thus what we have done is create a starting point for what we may look like if we so choose.

Now, let's examine the list again. How many of the traits listed are acquirable by us and how many are we born with? I believe we can agree that all the characteristics can be acquired through moral courage, self-discipline, and hard work. My question now is, if these traits are all acquirable and we agree that they are noble, virtuous, and highly admired, what prevents us from obtaining them? If we are honest with ourselves, we will admit the constraining influence is ourselves.

Finally, let's take a look at the list a third time and ask ourselves the question: What traits would we remove from the list for an effective follower? In all probability, none of the traits will be removed, thus what has been created is not the perfect leader model but rather the perfect leader/follower model.

The perfect leader and the perfect follower have identical traits, so what or who determines the leader? The leader is not the person with the title; rather the leader is that person who has the idea or experiences and the ability to influence others to follow. On a healthy, functioning team, leadership will tend to shift smoothly among team members depending upon the situation or who has the idea or specific experience.

I believe it is safe to say if we were to create a second model illustrating the characteristics of a person whom we would not follow with head, heart, and hands, we would create exactly the opposite set of characteristics. For example, if we admire humility then the opposite would be arrogance, integrity versus lack of integrity, self-centered versus selfless, and so on. Following the principle that two opposites cannot dwell in our mind at the same time, we simply choose what we do not desire and replace it with what we do desire.

DETERMINING OUR LOCATION

The beginning of *Navigating Change* is to know who we are. I like Plato's quote, "The unexamined life is not worth the living." Shakespeare said, "To thine own self be true." It seems to me nonsensical to believe that we could begin a journey without knowing our location and possessing the moral courage to examine ourselves honestly and realistically.

The reality of life's journey is there is always a gap between where we are and the dream of our possibilities. Just as in navigating through the forest, we must first examine ourselves. The following ideas can be helpful in determining where we are:

- Use the leader/follower model and add to it whatever additional traits are desired.

- Use the model as a benchmark to measure yourself.

- Take a credible personality-preference sorter of some kind. This could be DISC, Meyer Briggs, or others.

- Use a credible three-hundred-and-sixty degree survey to obtain feedback from your spouse, associates, boss, friends.

- Examine the condition of all relationships, personal and professional.

- Examine the status of your spiritual life and beliefs.

- Examine the general physical condition you are in. What kind of diet? Physical exercise?

- Examine your career path and job situation. Where is it and where is it going?

- Examine your intellectual life. How are you spending your time? How much TV time? What are you reading?

- Seek feedback from friends and associates. Be open and non-defensive.

- Begin to process the question: What is my purpose and why do I exist?

- Begin to think about your core values. What values do you have that are non-negotiable, unchanging, and not for sale at any price?

• Obtain a journal and begin to write about your thoughts, ambitions, emotions, and possibilities.

In short, attempt to accumulate information about who we are, not only in our own eyes but also in the eyes of others. As Plato said, "Seek to know yourself." It is only through honest, tough evaluation of our current location that we can begin the process to determine where we want to go and, then, how we will get there. This will be a lifetime journey we embark upon, sometimes painful, as we seek to discover who we are. The chances are high we will come upon many things we want to change.

I like this quote from Thomas Merton, who said, "It is in deep solitude that I find the gentleness with which I can truly love my brothers …Solitude and silence teach me to love my brothers for what they are, not what they say."

Remember the principle: **PEOPLE DO NOT CHANGE UNTIL THE PAIN OF NOT CHANGING IS GREATER THAN THE PAIN OF CHANGING.** We do not change until we see the need for change, and seeing the reason for personal change is something we do a great job of deluding ourselves about. There is a payoff for taking this leap from the "comfort zone." The payoff is that we grow, mature, and find that our relationships and life simply work better.

KNOW YOUR CURRENT LOCATION - KEY POINTS

• It is a fundamental navigational principle to know our location.

• We consist of three interdependent components: body, mind, and soul.

• The soul is the seat of our belief system and is where change must take place.

• A person does not change until the pain of not changing is greater than the pain of changing.

• We think and subsequently act in accordance with our innermost belief system.

• Moral and ethical behavior is learned and is a choice.

• An effective leader and follower have similar characteristics and traits.

• The beginning of navigating change is to know oneself.

• We are embarked on a lifetime journey of change and personal growth.

KEY PRINCIPLES

• If the soul is the seat of our belief systems and functions as our software then the mind represents the computer or hardware and the body the printer. It is the software that we must change.

- Thoughts and beliefs become energized when we dwell on them repeatedly and allow them to form a specific and clear attitude. The more energy we put into it, the deeper it becomes imbedded, and the more difficult it is to root out.

- In its simplest form, life is about having a personal compass consisting of purpose, values, and vision that align us. A compass that we believe in and are committed to is our tool for making reasoned choices about how we react to our circumstances.

KEY QUESTIONS

- What are the prerequisites to change?

- One of the laws of nature is that we can only think one thing at a time. If this is true, do you agree that what you think is what you are and will become? Does it follow that, for change to take place, it must happen in your belief systems and, therefore, your thought life?

- Create a model of the person you would follow with head, heart, and hands.

DETERMINE YOUR DESTINATION

And as soon as you have renounced that aim of "surviving at any price," and gone where the calm and simple people go — then imprisonment begins to transform your former character in an astonishing way. Once upon a time you were sharply intolerant. You were constantly in a rush. And you were constantly short of time. And now you have time with interest ... its months and its years, behind you and ahead of you — and a beneficial calming fluid pours through your blood vessels — patience. Formerly you never forgave anyone. You judged people without mercy. And you praised people with equal lack of moderation ...You have come to realize your own weakness — and you can therefore understand the weakness of others. And be astonished at another's strength. And wish to possess it yourself. The stones rustle beneath our feet. We are ascending.

- Aleksandr Solzhenitsyn
The Gulag Archipelago

It seems to me a fairly common sense proposition that in order to reach our destination we need to know what it is. As the Cheshire cat said to Alice, "If you don't know where you want to go, then either road will do." It is nonsensical to think otherwise, thus a basic tenet of navigation is determining our destination, that is, where do we want to be when we arrive where we are going.

To repeat, the topographical map represents us with all our skills, abilities, beliefs, experiences, personality, and intelligence, a valuable pool of attributes. In order to orient the map, we lay the compass on top of it and turn the bezel to a parallel position to the perpendicular lines on the map. After we have done this, we turn our bodies until the red arrow on the compass is aligned with the arrow on the bezel.

Our map has now been oriented with our compass with the top of the map pointing toward the north, the bottom south, left side west, and right side pointing to the east. We now rotate our bodies to the side of the map opposite to that which we want to look. What we are looking for should be right in front of us. Without this orientation process, we can never be sure if our map is pointed in the right direction. Now what's the point?

The point is that this metaphor of map and compass is directly related to us. The principle is that a map, not properly oriented, has little value in getting us to our desired destination. If we expect to arrive at our desired destination, we need to know what and where it is and be on the correct and true road to get there. The compass is the tool allowing us to do this.

The third precept in Navigating Change is to determine our destination. Our destination is reflected in our compass and consists of three components: Core Purpose, Core Values, and Vision.

CORE PURPOSE

One of the greatest sources of anxiety, restlessness, and feeling too busy is a lack of personal meaning and purpose. Such a condition results in a tendency to seek after external satisfaction and stimulation versus internal purpose. To establish meaning and purpose in our life is to discover our soul.

What is "life purpose"? If we search inside ourselves, it is something we need in order to feel complete, whole, and fulfilled in our life. It must be internally generated and answers the question, "Why do we exist?"

The interesting paradox about the discovery of life purpose is it is generally "other-directed," having an impact on someone or something other than ourself. This introduces the principle of attraction. We tend to attract that which we are and give away. If we want to be loved then we must love. If we want to be encouraged, we must be an encourager; if we desire to be listened to, we must become good listeners. If we desire peace with our self and influence with others then we must have a core purpose.

Every person must come to terms with themselves as to their core purpose. This involves the moral courage to look inward and define with clarity why we exist. This is a process that each person must traverse individually, and each of us may view our purpose as different than others. I have painfully worked through this process myself and concluded that my purpose in life is to be a servant or, as Plumb calls it, a parachute packer in order to honor the God I serve. I believe the determination of core purpose is the most important one an individual or an organization will make. Purpose will provide the passion and the peace we desire to make our lives fulfilled and complete.

Life purpose should not change and should never be fully actualized.

That would represent the perfection that we are not capable of reaching. Neither should life purpose be confused with goals, strategies, or objectives. These will change and adjust as experience and circumstances dictate. Purpose, however, remains constant, representing a future perfect state we desire to fulfill. A constant purpose is like a compass in that, while it does not change, it inspires change. Seeking after purpose is one of the components enabling us to stay on the right course regardless of the circumstances.

STEPS TO DETERMINING CORE PURPOSE

Sit down quietly with journal and pen or pencil and answer the following questions:

- What do I want to do with my life?

- Why is this important to know?

- Would others notice if I ceased to exist?

- What purpose do I serve in the lives of other people?

- What is my life dedicated to?

- What would family, friends, and associates say about me if I died today?

- Do I have fulfillment in my profession, relationships, spiritual and physical life?

- What am I passionate about?

Finally, conduct a "purpose tournament" with yourself using the following guidelines:

- Make a list of your top eight needs, passions, or desires in each of four categories: physical, relationships, intellectual (professional), and spiritual.

- You will have created four groups of eight items each (total of thirty-two).

- Create a single-elimination tournament bracket for each category, i.e. physical, relationships, intellectual, and spiritual.

- Pair off your top eight items and conduct a tournament with the top need, as you determine it, advancing in the tournament until you have a final winner in each category. If you have done this thoughtfully, the results should be very revealing to you as to where your passions are.

- Now have a final four tournament with the winners of each category. This will give you a champion, that need, desire, or passion you deem the most important of all things in your life.

- Compare your final four category champions with the questions you answered in the previous exercise. Are they consistent? Different? How?

Now it is time to write your purpose statement. The purpose statement should capture the essence of who you desire to become and what you desire to do with the rest of your life. This statement should not necessarily reflect where you are, rather what it is you desire to become. It should be a maximum of two sentences long. As you go through this exercise, keep in mind that core purpose is not a goal or an objective (these can be adjusted); it is a future perfect state that is unlikely to change or ever be reached perfectly.

CORE VALUES

A value is that quality of a thing which is thought of as useful, valuable, and important. Values are worthy of esteem for their own sake and have intrinsic worth as guides or standards for our life. Core values are those we hold so deeply that they are simply not negotiable or for sale at any price. No set of circumstances can warrant or justify the violation of a core value. Core values are different than simple values. For instance, integrity or honesty or 100% Responsibility might be core values, while playing golf once a week might be a value. The difference between the two, obviously, is that one set should not change while the other can.

Core values are essential tenets that provide the foundational basis for how we live our lives. They are fundamental, deeply held, and seldom, if ever, change.

STEPS TO DETERMINING CORE VALUES

• Sit down with journal and pen and or pencil.

• Make a list of ten core values as defined above.

- Reduce the number to five.

- Ask yourself, What is the most important thing in my life? Second? Third?

- Do my actions support my core values?

- What would I tell my spouse or children that my values are?

- If I had all the money I would ever need, would I have the same values?

- Will my values be the same twenty years from now as they are today?

- Would I hold to these values even if I had to suffer financially or otherwise?

- Are there any circumstances that would justify my violation of these values?

If we cannot answer yes to the last six questions then the values we have listed are not core values. A core value should never be changed due to circumstances. Core values should be consistent regardless of the confusion, chaos, unfairness, or ambiguity we may find ourselves in.

As a guideline, I give you my personal core values:

- 100% Responsibility

- Integrity

- Commitment To Truth

- Continual Growth

- Love and Honor Others

- Excellence In All That I Do

Do not confuse core values with strategies, objectives, or goals. If you have been honest with yourself, you have created a set of core values of five to seven that you can commit to.

VISION

There is a Chinese proverb that says, "Unless you change direction in your life you are likely to arrive at where you are headed."

This proverb aptly characterizes the obvious and illustrates the importance of having a desired end state we want to reach. Vision is a future perfect state that is credible, realistic, and attractive. Vision does not outline how we will get to our destination, only how we will look when we arrive.

Vision, unlike core purpose or core values, can change and be adjusted based upon experience, opportunities, etc. It is the creation of a picture or photograph of what we can possibly look like at some future determined time, providing us with inspiration and encouragement to persevere in its attainment. A carefully thought-out vision empowers us to take action.

What we earnestly strive to bring about tends to become reality over time, if we persevere. A vision infuses us with possibilities measuring the height of our aim, the range of our efficiency.   Our vision is a mental picture of the possible, and men and women who vigorously pursue it will achieve those heights of which they dream.

DEVELOPING A VISION

- Sit down with journal and pen or pencil

- Have in front of me my core purpose and core values.

- Have in front of me my tournament of purpose.

- Divide my vision into four parts: Physical, Intellectual, Emotional, and Spiritual.

- Have a five-year time horizon.

- In each part, dream and think about what I want to look like in five years.

- What do I want to look like physically? Weight? Diet? Exercise? Activities?

- What do I want to look like intellectually? Professionally? Books read? School or academic courses taken?

- What do I want my relationships to look like? Spouse, children, grandchildren, business associates, friends, others? Is there any one against whom I harbor anger or bitterness that might restrict me?

- What do I want to look like spiritually? Daily quiet time? Bible or inspirational book study? Church, synagogue, or other attendance? Relationship with God?

- Think about these areas and write one paragraph on each. See yourself as accomplishing those things you include in your paragraph. We cannot become something we first do not think about.

- Now write one paragraph that pulls together all four areas.

This paragraph, to be a driving and empowering force, must elicit passion, enthusiasm, and commitment. This vision, along with core purpose and core values, is what will provide the direction to our life. It is our compass that, when used to orient our map, keeps our course true. The compass is the tool that can be used to help us make choices and set priorities, keeping all our abilities and talents focused on being the right kind of person.

I like the quote by Albert Einstein, who said, "Try not to become men and women of success but instead strive to be men and women of value." Clarity of purpose, values, and vision is what guides us on this journey.

DETERMINE YOUR DESTINATION - KEY POINTS

- A basic tenet of navigation is to know our destination.

- Our destination is our compass, consisting of purpose, values, and vision.

- We navigate by aligning our map with our compass.

- One of the greatest sources of anxiety is a lack of personal purpose and meaning.

- Conducting a purpose tournament can help provide direction.

- Core values are tenets we hold so deeply as to direct all our behaviors.

- Core purpose is the fundamental reason for our existence.

- Vision is the future perfect state we desire: physically, spiritually, intellectually, and emotionally.

KEY PRINCIPLES

- Fundamental to arriving at our destination is to know where it is we wish to be when we arrive there.

- If our map is not oriented properly, with the top of the map always pointing to the north, then we will never be looking at what we think we are looking at.

- The interesting paradox about core purpose is that it is generally "other-directed," having an impact on someone or something other than oneself.

- Core values and core purpose are neither negotiable nor for sale. Circumstances should never determine our reactions; rather it is our purpose and values that determine our actions and responses.

KEY QUESTIONS

- What is your core purpose? Why do you exist on this earth?

- What are your core values? Are these subject to the situation or are they not for sale?

- Do you agree that core purpose should never be realized? Why or why not?

- Albert Einstein said, "Try not to become men of success but instead men of value." What does he mean by this statement?

ORIENT YOUR MAP AND COMPASS

The greatest way to live with honor in this life is to be what we pretend to be.

- Socrates

Self-esteem is basically the opinion and regard in which we hold ourselves. Many people will argue that self-esteem is primarily determined by our environment and external influences. To buy into this approach, however, flies in the face of 100% Responsibility and other precepts we have talked about. To think that other people are in control of our opinions of self empowers them and not us.

Turning over this control to others is "prison thinking," "victim thinking," and "stinking thinking." I define self-esteem as making a promise to myself and keeping that promise. Thus, whenever I make a promise to myself and violate that promise, I am violating my personal integrity, and my opinion of myself is lowered. If I continue to violate my personal integrity by breaking promises to myself, I cause the demise of my self-esteem. Conversely, if I keep promises to myself, my opinion of myself will increase.

Navigating Change is about keeping promises and commitments to self and, as a result, maintaining personal integrity. The irony is that we keep promises to others before we keep them to ourselves.

I believe we cannot consistently maintain integrity in our interaction with others unless we are first maintaining integrity with ourselves. The most important person to have a commitment to truth and integrity with is that person we see in the mirror each morning.

Violating personal integrity is the most damaging thing we can do to ourselves and is the root cause of virtually every addiction. What is integrity? **INTEGRITY BEGINS WITH A COMMITMENT TO MYSELF TO ADHERE TO MY CORE PURPOSE AND CORE VALUES REGARDLESS OF THE CIRCUMSTANCES.**

The word integrity is derived from the root word "integer," a mathematical term meaning anything complete in itself, e.g. a whole number or zero as distinguished from a fraction or part of a whole number. As this applies to us, it means we are single-minded as opposed to double-minded; what we say is what we do, etc. We are trustworthy in terms of character and competence. We are who we say we are, lacking any duplicity. Integrity is actually an engineering term meaning that an object, building, etc. does what it was designed to do. If a bridge over the Mississippi River is designed to withstand one-hundred-mile-an-hour winds, high water, and a collision with a thirty-barge tow then, if it has integrity, the bridge will hold when tested by these circumstances. If the bridge lacks integrity, it will fracture and collapse. Integrity is a commonly used word by engineers as they define the characteristics of something they design.

There is a difference between knowing about integrity and actually acting with integrity. Integrity is not only saying we have integrity but also doing the right thing regardless of the circumstances. I have heard integrity described as "what you do when no one else is looking." Neither is integrity relative to the situation. There are no degrees of integrity. We either have it or we do not.

Integrity, like attitude, is not determined by circumstances but rather revealed by them. When we are squeezed, under pressure in a difficult situation, then we will reveal whether we have integrity or not, e.g. when the decision is unpopular or when there is a personal risk in doing the right thing.

Remember the movie *Hoosiers*, a story about a small-town high school basketball team in Hickory, Indiana? A new coach arrives, Norman Dale, with a storied past of winning at any cost. Coach Dale starts with six players of dubious ability joined later by a seventh player, Jimmie, who turns out to be the star player.

Coach Dale institutes strict discipline including a controversial practice he calls the "four pass" rule. The unpopular rule requires four passes among team members before a shot could be taken at the basket. The town people are suspect of the newcomer's methods, particularly the strong discipline and the "four pass" rule. After one of his players violates the rule, Dale benches him. Then another player fouls out, reducing the court players to four. Dale refuses to return the benched player to the game, finishing the game with four players and losing the game, causing even more pressure from the fans.

Why did Coach Dale stick to his methods under this kind of pressure? Because he knew there was a principle at work that would not only produce a better team but also character and discipline in his players. Dale risked losing and popularity and acted with personal integrity by adhering to his core values and core purpose

The payoff for Dale's character as exhibited to his players is that they showed their integrity through hard work and perseverance and became the kind of team Dale wanted. The team then continued on to the Indiana State Championship, winning against a much bigger city high school team. Even though the team went on to win the state title, the real winners were the players themselves, who benefited the rest of their lives from what Dale taught them.

Navigating Change demands personal integrity. Let's not delude ourselves. If we lie and break promises to that person we see in the mirror each morning, we are not keeping promises to anyone else. Others will sense our duplicity and our influence with them will wane. Personal integrity relates directly to everything we do and is, in fact, the fiber running through the fabric of our life.

Personal integrity dictates that every time we have a choice to make, circumstances are difficult, and the pressure is on us, we must adhere to our commitment to our core values and core purpose. Our map may be screaming to take us in a different direction, away from our destination, and this is when the compass must be used to calmly lay upon the face of the map and turn it in the right direction. The compass needle never lies, it always points north, providing us with the objective and unemotional guide we need to navigate through the forests of life.

KNOW YOUR CURRENT LOCATION - KEY POINTS

- Self-esteem is the opinion and regard we hold for ourselves.

- When we violate a promise to ourselves, we violate our personal integrity.

- The most important person to maintain a commitment to is self.

- Integrity comes from the root word "integer," meaning whole, indivisible.

- There are no degrees of integrity; we either have it or we do not.

- Integrity is being aligned with our core purpose and core values.

- Like attitude, integrity is revealed by circumstances, not determined by them.

- Navigating Change demands personal integrity, doing what we say we will do.

- Integrity relates to everything and is the thread running through our life's fabric.

KEY PRINCIPLES

- If we are not keeping promises to the person we see in the mirror each morning then we are not keeping promises to others. We cannot maintain integrity with others if we are not maintaining integrity with ourselves.

- Integrity begins with a commitment to oneself to adhere to a core purpose and core values regardless of the circumstances.

- There is a difference between knowing about integrity and acting with integrity. It is not only saying we are trustworthy but also acting as if we are trustworthy, regardless of the situation.

KEY QUESTIONS

- Socrates said, "The greatest way to live with honor in this life is to be what we pretend to be." What does he mean by this?

- Do you agree that integrity is internally generated and not subject to external circumstances?

- Do you keep promises to yourself? How do you feel about yourself when you break a promise? Do you agree that personal integrity is the key to self-esteem?

DEVELOP AN INCREMENTAL PLAN

Conviction is worthless unless it is converted into conduct.

- Thomas Carlyle

We are still sitting on that trail, under the canopy of forest, working our navigation model, determined to survive and thrive. We have an attitude of positive expectation, seeing our lost situation as an opportunity to learn. We have determined our current location and destination on our topographical map, and we have oriented the map with the compass. The top of the map is pointing to the north, and, as we look ahead of us, we can see with clarity those physical features of terrain that are also present on the map. Our confidence is growing.

We can see there is a gap between where we are and where we want to go. It is now time to develop an incremental plan on how we will get there. A key navigation principle is that the shortest distance between two points is not always the fastest. In fact, my own experience in the woods has shown me this is almost always the case. Why? Because in difficult wilderness terrain, there are many obstacles, such as mountains, gorges, rivers, and anything that slows us or prevents us from traveling in a straight line to our destination.

In traveling this journey, we must make an incremental plan based upon data provided by our map, compass, and our reasoned judgment as to the most effective and productive route to travel. These reasoned choices would be based upon our resources, physical and mental fitness, protection, food and water sources, safety, and obstacles. All these factors would be weighed as we develop our plan.

Why an incremental plan? By incremental, we mean a plan set forth as a series made up of small pieces leading to a whole. Incremental planning is important for several reasons:

- Allows us to plan in known pieces. We usually know more about the first piece of the plan than we do of those farther down the trail.

- Allows us to be more flexible. We can change and adjust faster if we are planning in increments.

- Gives us quicker warning when we are off course. The smaller the planning increment, the sooner we will know if we are drifting or have made the wrong plan to begin with.

- Allows us to collect features as we go. (More on this in next chapter)

- Builds our confidence.

Developing an incremental plan should not preclude us from having a plan for the entire route. An incremental plan simply recognizes that larger plans are likely to change as more information and experience is gathered. For example, we may plan to move down a trail a few hundred meters to a road, this being the first increment, and then proceed down the road an additional few hundred meters to a trailhead. As we commence the third increment, we are headed to a creek. Upon reaching the creek, we find it has been swollen with recent rains and cannot be crossed at this location. Now we must sit down with our map and compass and reevaluate our plan.

Creating an action plan for oneself is no different. We must plan in increments, based upon what we know and the resources we have. We should anticipate change and obstacles and be willing to be flexible, making adjustments as we go.

It is okay to change strategies, tactics, goals, objectives, etc. as circumstances change. Thus an action plan is always in some state of flux and tweaking as we are confronted with new circumstances. What does not change, however, is our personal compass. Our personal compass, consisting of core values, core purpose, and vision, rarely, if ever, changes.

HEALTHY TENSION

There always will be a tension between the reality of our current situation and our personal compass. This tension is, in fact, healthy – provided it is making us sharper rather than duller. There is a proverb that says, "As iron sharpens iron so one man sharpens another." When a knife is sharpened, both heat and sparks are produced, but the result is a sharper instrument. This underscores the value of self-evaluation and feedback from others we trust. The essence of personal mastery is learning how to balance the creative tension of reality in our life with the objective, relentless compass needle always pointing us in the right direction.

LEARNING

Learning, in this context, does not mean that we simply acquire knowledge about ourselves. It means expanding our ability to produce the results, in terms of behavior change and actions we desire. We have not learned anything until we actually put into practice knowledge we have gained. Personal mastery of that person we look at in the mirror each morning implies a craftsman-like skill in continually honing our character and competence in all areas of our life: physically, emotionally, intellectually, and spiritually.

AN INDIVIDUAL OF PERSONAL MASTERY WILL:

- Live their life with no excuses nor blame

- Embrace all change as an opportunity to learn and grow

- Be committed to the truth

- Accept current reality and control their reaction to it

- Be balanced in all areas of their life

- Have a clear sense of core purpose

- Live by a set of core values

- Have clarity of vision

- View life as a continual learning process

- Influence but not control others

LIVING IN THE PRESENT

Our goal should be to continually live in the present. We should focus on doing those things that promote our core purpose and desired end state consistent and aligned with our core values. In order to live in the present, we must release the past and not be afraid of the future. As Einstein said, "Try to become men and women of value."

BALANCE

We are a system made up of four parts. We have physical, mental, emotional, and spiritual dimensions. All these parts are interdependent and must work together to produce healthy living, thinking, and synergy. If one is out of balance, the odds are high that all are out of balance. The more in balance these four areas of our life are, the more purpose, passion, and peace will be experienced.

BUILDING AN INCREMENTAL PLAN

- Sit down with journal and a pen or pencil.

- Have in front of me my core purpose statement.

- Have in front of me my core values.

- Have in front of me my vision statement.

- Have in front of me my purpose tournament.

- Using the champion from each bracket, i.e. physical, spiritual, etc., create a total of twelve actionable items, three for each of the four categories. These need to be specific and measurable.

- Time span on these twelve actionable items is twelve months.

- Determine who is responsible for accomplishing the twelve action items.

- What is the schedule for their completion?

- How will I know I am on target?

- Who will hold me accountable?

- How often will I review my progress on these items?

RELATIONSHIPS

One of the key factors in arriving at real peace with purpose in our lives is the honest evaluation of our relationships with others. I believe we only have as much peace in our life as our worst relationship. Think for a moment about someone we hold some degree of anger or root of bitterness toward and how much time we spend thinking about that situation or person. If we are honest with ourselves, we will admit we spend an inordinate amount of energy on those things or people who irritate us versus what we do on relationships we enjoy and are at peace with. For example, if we have ten key relationships and one is bad and nine are good, I would bet we spend more time thinking about the bad one than the other nine combined.

Part of our action plan is to make amends to and peace with anyone we are angry with or bitter toward. Difficult? Scary? Absolutely! However, to grow and achieve purpose and peace in our lives, we must resolve all issues to the extent that we have control over them. Fear and pride constrain us and hold us in bondage as sure as Plumb in his physical prison cell. As long as we harbor anger, hatred, bitterness, or jealousy, we are in bondage to that person or circumstance.

If these things are not cleaned up and amends made, then no amount of good planning can overcome them. Is this fair? No, this is freedom! The reason we make amends, regardless of what the other person may have done, is for our benefit, not theirs. We cannot control how other people will respond, but we have total control over what we do. Remember Viktor Frankl's comment: "The last of one's freedoms is to choose how I will respond to what you have done to me."

FREEDOM FROM THE BONDAGE OF FEELINGS
AND EMOTIONS REQUIRES ME TO:

• Admit to myself my feelings of anger and bitterness

• Release blame and excuses involving that person

• Take 100% Responsibility for what I can do about the situation

• Go to that person and ask for forgiveness for my anger toward them

• Release any expectation that the other person will acknowledge their complicity

• If they do, accept their apology with grace and humility

The worst case in this situation is that we are free. The best case is that we are free, the other person is free, and we have a mended and functioning relationship again. In either case, we are ready to move on with our action plan without the constraints of emotional leg-irons and prison bars.

WARNING

I cannot emphasize enough the importance of maintaining healthy relationships with everyone, as far as what we can do is concerned. There is nothing more debilitating than anger and bitterness toward others. Remember the principle that we can only think one thing at a time and that we tend to attract what we are. Therefore love attracts love, hatred attracts hatred. We cannot be something different than we think in our heart and mind anymore than we can expect to harvest corn where squash was sown. That would be to visit the realm of insanity.

DEVELOP AN INCREMENTAL PLAN - KEY POINTS

- There is always a gap between where we are and where we want to go.

- The shortest distance between two points is not always the fastest.

- Planning in increments allows flexibility and gives us quicker warning when we are off course.

- Our plan should cover all components of who we are and desire to be: physically, spiritually, intellectually, and emotionally.

- Changing strategy and tactics as we travel is expected as situations warrant.

- There will always be a tension between the reality of our situation and our compass.

- An important part of our incremental plan is always keeping our relationships in order.

KEY PRINCIPLES

• We only have as much peace in our lives as our worst relationship. Taking 100% Responsibility for maintaining good relationships with everyone is what provides the energy we need to focus on positive growth.

• An incremental plan must be consistent and always aligned with our personal compass. It is the compass that keeps our map oriented in the right direction.

• We reap that which we sow later than we sow and more than we sow. An incremental plan aligned with our compass is what keeps us planting that which we desire to reap and not allowing the weeds to overrun our garden.

KEY QUESTIONS

• What does the statement "We sow our wild oats and then pray for crop failure" mean to you?

• Do you have any relationships that you harbor anger, bitterness, resentment, jealousy, or other emotions in?

• What do you intend to do about those relationships? Whose responsibility is it to do something about them? Who benefits?

COLLECT FEATURES AS YOU GO

Many persons have a wrong ideal of what constitutes true happiness. It is not attained through self-gratification but through fidelity to a purpose.

\- Helen Keller

It is time to commence our journey. We are no longer lost. Although our circumstances have not changed, our attitude and self-confidence has. We have positive expectations, know our location and destination, have oriented our map and compass, and developed an incremental plan to get there. We now move on to the trail and begin the journey.

Remember the enemy Pogo warned us about? "I have seen the enemy and he is me" should warn us as to the major problem, ourselves. It is our perception of reality and our belief system that we must guard against; thoughts, emotions, and negative self-talk that can divert us and take us off in a direction we do not wish to travel.

Trails tend to follow terrain contour lines. A contour line is indicated on our topographical map as a brown, squiggly line that seems to randomly wander everywhere. If we follow along this brown line, we will find a number that indicates the elevation this line runs along. A contour line follows a constant terrain elevation, thus its squiggly route. The difference between each brown line represents a twenty-foot difference in elevation. The wider the lines are apart, the flatter the terrain and, conversely, the narrower the lines, the steeper.

Since trails and roads tend to follow terrain contour lines, it follows that the trails themselves also twist and turn in a random manner. For example, we are on a trail heading south, and, fifty meters down the trail, it bends to the west and then back to the north, east, and so on. These shifts in trail direction are many times so subtle as to be undetectable by us. If we are not collecting features as we travel, we will find ourselves drifting off course, and the further we drift without detection, the more off course we become.

What does it mean to collect features as you go? A feature on a topographical map is literally anything of note as indicated by a symbol for its existence. For example, a feature could be any of the following:

- Trails, roads, or highways

- Power lines

- Buildings or bridges

- Forests or clearings

- Mountains, valleys, or gorges

- Lakes, rivers, ponds, or creeks

- Terrain contour lines at constant elevations

- Airports, dams, or power stations

Virtually any symbol on the topographical map can qualify as a feature. As we navigate on our journey through the wilderness, collecting features is what confirms for us that we are heading toward our desired destination. If we see on our map that a trail should be heading to lower elevations and we are going down hill, we have collected a feature. Crossing a creek, power line, or road enables us to collect a feature confirming where we are. A trail bending to the west when it is supposed to is also a collected feature.

The precept of collecting features applies to life just as surely. It is situational awareness or constant vigilance of changes or markers that confirm for us our course. The presence of features sought confirms our path while features found but not expected cause us to pause and evaluate our situation and location.

MAINTAINING OUR COURSE:

- Have a daily quiet time to reflect, order the day, and be inspired.

- Process our thoughts and emotions: Are they negative? In error? Unrealistic? Rebellious? Obsessed? Enslaved?

- Resolve conflicts with win-win attitude.

- Maintain expectations agreements, doing what we say we will do.

- Have a regular accountability partner who cares about us enough to ask the tough questions.

- Maintain "positive relationship accounts" with everyone with whom we interact.

- Make every choice in alignment with core purpose and core values.

- Allow no excuses, blaming, whining, or rationalizing.

- Be committed to the truth.

- Maintain an attitude of gratefulness and prayer.

- Order priorities, preventing the good squeezing out the best.

CONCENTRATION

Management guru Peter Drucker said, "If there is any one 'secret' of effectiveness, it is concentration. Effective executives (people) do first things first and they do one thing at a time."

Drucker has touched the key to maintaining our course. In the process of becoming the persons we desire to become, we must be sure to order our priorities. Ordering priorities is what keeps us pursuing the best rather than being bogged down by the good. The good is the enemy of the best.

How do we do this? As Drucker points out, we focus on first things first:

- Keep priorities simple.

- There should be a few priorities in each category: physical, intellectual, emotional, and spiritual.

- Priorities should flow from vision and action plan.

- Priorities should be consistent with core values.

- Priorities should align with core purpose.

- Carry out priorities one at a time.

- Priorities should be done weekly and tweaked daily.

A principle at work is that if we do not set priorities then circumstances or others will set them for us. Peace is a gift that flows when we are involved in right thinking and have our priorities balanced and in order.

> *Only by their actions can a person make themselves and their life whole...we are responsible for what we have done and the people who we have influenced.*
>
> - Margaret Bourke-White

EXPECTATIONS AGREEMENT

One of the most fundamental precepts of a relationship is a shared expectation. This simple precept is perhaps one of the most violated and potentially destructive in our relationships with one another.

Because of our personality preferences and life experiences, we tend to receive, process, and internalize information in different ways. We listen to or view the same information and come to different conclusions in different time frames. Differing perspectives is positive and brings richness and synergy in our relationships with each other. They are also the source of misunderstanding and tension and can, however unintentionally, be the source of mistrust.

Trust does not occur by accident but rather is earned by keeping promises and doing what we say we will do when we say we will do it. We are 100% Responsible for maintaining trust in our relationships by being trustworthy people. If we are trustworthy both in character and competence then we will be trusted; if we are not trustworthy then we will not be trusted.

There is a big payoff for trust. Relationships work better, they are more effective and productive, and energies are devoted to solving problems rather than being the problem. Trust is basic to healthy win-win relationships and will grow as it is exercised. A model I use to provide structure in my agreements is as follows:

- I MAKE ONLY AGREEMENTS I INTEND TO KEEP.

- I AVOID MAKING OR ACCEPTING "FUZZY" AGREEMENTS.

- I GIVE EARLIEST NOTICE WHEN AGREEMENTS CANNOT BE KEPT.

- I CLEAN UP BROKEN AGREEMENTS.

Making "fuzzy" agreements tends to be a problem for many of us. This is because we don't like structured time and, at the same time, we don't want to hurt people's feelings. As a result, we sometimes make agreements that are vague and nebulous, e.g. "Let's have lunch sometime."

The problem, of course, with a "fuzzy" agreement is that it can create an expectation of one of the parties when the other party meant no such commitment. The result? Mistrust! The bottom line in any relationship is clear, unambiguous communication using the five Ws of journalism: who, what, when, where, and why. We simply avoid making any agreement that we do not fully intend to keep.

Sometimes we cannot keep an agreement we have entered into in good faith. When this occurs, we must have the courtesy and courage to advise as soon as possible that the agreement cannot be kept. Waiting until the last moment to break an agreement we knew could not be kept exhibits a lack of integrity and produces mistrust in the other party.

When an agreement is broken, we must clean it up as soon as possible. We do this by taking 100% Responsibility; the other party is not interested in excuses and blame. Then we ask for forgiveness and, if applicable, attempt to reschedule the commitment. Living our life with expectation agreements is a key to the purpose, passion, and peace that we seek.

MAINTAINING POSITIVE-BALANCE RELATIONSHIP ACCOUNTS

An important tool for maintaining relationships is the relationship account. Whether we realize it or not, we open a relationship account with virtually everyone we come in contact with from the cashier at the supermarket to the important client we are trying to build a relationship with to our spouse and children.

The relationship account functions much like a bank checking account in that both deposits and withdrawals are made. We understand this principle very well in the financial world. If we deposit money into our account then we are entitled to withdraw up to the amount of money we have in the account. A fundamental governing principle is that something cannot be created from nothing. If there is nothing in our account then nothing can be withdrawn. This is not hard to understand.

Healthy, functioning relationships require positive balances. Positive balances in the relationship are what enable the parties to give and take and build trust with one another. What is a deposit and withdrawal? I have a list I use:

DEPOSITS

- Listening

- Words of encouragement

- Letters or notes of encouragement

- Special recognition or rewards

- Having a special vision for others

- Doing what we say we will do

- Being trustworthy

- Meaningful and appropriate touch

- Including others in what is going on

- Asking the opinion of others

WITHDRAWALS

- Interrupting

- Sidebar conversations

- Excluding others

- Not doing what we say we will do

- Taking credit for something someone else did

- Dishonesty

- Rudeness and lack of common courtesy

- Not asking the opinion of others

- Lack of punctuality

When we look at the list of deposits and withdrawals, they all tie back into the highest needs that each of us have:

- The need to love or be loved

- The need to be understood

- The need to be important, valuable, and significant

The driving principle behind the relationship account is that **PEOPLE DO NOT CARE WHAT WE KNOW UNTIL THEY KNOW THAT WE CARE**. A burgeoning account with another person determines the level of trust and commitment put forth. We want to commit to something greater than ourselves, to be a part of something that has purpose and value; a full account facilitates this commitment.

THE WEB OF CONSEQUENCES

We make choices daily, hopefully with as much reasoned thought as possible, trying to sort out the consequences of our decisions. Because we normally have a number of possible options to choose from, it is difficult to anticipate the intended and unintended implications of them all. The Web of Consequences is a good tool to use in our decision-making process.

The benefits of the Web are that it allows us to begin with a core problem we are attempting to solve and then track the various options, possibilities, and consequences. We can assess negative and positive outcomes to the options and clearly see how they connect with one another. It helps us anticipate outcomes and stay focused on the problem. It can be used for virtually any personal or organizational decision confronting us.

To use the Web, there are certain guidelines to abide by:

- We begin with a large piece of flip-chart paper and several markers of different colors.

- We determine the core problem.

- We only use statements that have a possibility of happening.

- We do not argue or debate about the possibilities. Simply record them.

- We record negative and positive consequences for each possibility.

- We need to be as specific as possible.

- Do not be afraid of the obvious or the "way out" options.

- Record consequences in sequential order.

To begin, we need a clear and specific core problem as our Web center statement. For example: What are the consequences of my retirement at age fifty-five? Place the problem statement in the center of the flip-chart paper within a circle.

Now come up with five consequences of this possibility and place them in five circles around the center statement connected by lines. Examples might be: more leisure time, less money coming in, boredom, freedom to go back to school, etc. Give yourself about thirty minutes to do this and then score the consequences on a scale of plus five to minus five. Plus five would be extremely desirable at one extreme, and minus five would be extremely undesirable at the other.

After scoring the first tier, move to the second tier with five circles around each circle of the first tier. Each contains a possible consequence of the consequence. For example, the second tier of consequences of more leisure time could be a better golf game or reading more, writing a book, etc. Now score the second tier in the same manner as the first tier.

Move to the third tier and repeat again in the exact manner as the first and second tier of consequences. Score the third tier. We have now created the Web of Consequences, clarifying for us the various options with intended and unintended consequences identified. The Web does not make the decision for us but is a tool as we process the problems we encounter.

Collecting features helps us confirm our course and alert us to a drift from that course. This requires us to be constantly vigilant and aware of any changes in our situation. The tools provided in this chapter can help provide the needed situational awareness we need to correct and stay on our course.

COLLECT FEATURES AS YOU GO - KEY POINTS

- We are no longer lost and are ready to move out on our journey.

- A feature is any kind of landmark that will confirm our course for us.

- It is situational awareness of our surroundings that alerts us to danger.

- The presence of features sought confirms our path while features not looked for cause us to pause and evaluate our situation.

- We must continually process our thoughts and emotions.

- A daily quiet time with self is important to staying on course.

- Don't allow the good things to squeeze out the best.

- Maintain positive relationship accounts with everyone.

- Maintain expectation agreements in all we do.

KEY PRINCIPLES

- One of the most fundamental precepts of a relationship is a shared expectation. This simple precept is perhaps one of the most violated and potentially destructive in our relationships with one another.

- One of the laws of nature is that we cannot create something from nothing. This principle governs all our relationships in that we must maintain positive account balances with all those we wish to influence. Healthy, functioning relationships require positive balances.

- There are intended and unintended consequences for every action. Processing our decisions and choices before we carry them out saves us from heartache and mistakes.

KEY QUESTIONS

- Do you have a daily quiet time? Do you have an accountability partner?

- Do you maintain expectation agreements with family, friends, and associates?

- Pogo said, "I have seen the enemy and he is me." What does this mean to you?

HAVE A
STOPPING POINT

---

*Now, what should happen when you make a
mistake is this: You take your knocks, learn
your lessons, and then you move on. That's
the healthiest way to deal with a problem.*

- Ronald Reagan

The seventh and final precept of Navigating Change is: Have a stopping point! A stopping point is a designated feature beyond our desired destination that signals to us we have missed our mark. For example, we would look beyond our destination on the topographical map to find a prominent feature, e.g. a power line, creek, or road, to designate as a stopping point. If we reach the stopping point, we have overshot our target and need to regroup.

The precept of having a stopping point applies directly to how we navigate our own lives. Life is difficult, confusing, continually changing, and unfair. We stumble, fall, get off course, and regularly struggle as we move through it. This is the world we live in, and the only control we have over the situation is our reaction to it. Stopping points help us with the fact we are lost or have drifted off course, missing our intended mark.

STOPPING POINTS

There are three vehicles that I use for stopping points and have found a need for all of them. My first stopping point is my daily quiet time. This quiet time is the number one priority in my life, and I always have it early in the morning, lasting for fifteen minutes to sixty minutes or longer. I believe my life works better when I have this time alone.

HOT VERSUS COLD COFFEE

I like to visualize, so here is a metaphor for my quiet time experience. I love a hot cup of coffee in the morning and always fix myself a pot before I sit down alone. Sometime during my quiet time, I will get up and get a second cup but almost never finish it, usually leaving about a half of a cup. Occasionally, I will leave that cup of coffee on the table next to my chair and forget to take it to the kitchen.

When I return the following morning, I find the cup still there, but now it is cold, murky, dark, and bitter. It is not fit to drink. If I leave the cup there for a few more days, which I have done, and return, I will find not only the cup of coffee more bitter and murky but now sporting a growth of green mold. It is disgusting and difficult to even carry to the kitchen and wash out. The longer I leave the cup without cleaning it out, the worse it gets.

Get the picture? The cup represents me and the coffee is what I choose to pour into and keep in my cup. I understand myself well and know that, if I go more than twenty-four hours without dumping the garbage I have accumulated, I will be on the path to becoming just as bitter, dark, and cold as that cup of coffee. What kind of garbage? Any feelings or thoughts of anger, malice, jealousy, hatred, prejudice, or bitterness that I have, no matter how small, need to be admitted, rooted out, and released.

I have never failed to have something or someone I need to deal with. Many times, I have needed to make amends with someone and have gotten up from my quiet time and immediately called them, asking for forgiveness for something I have done or said. I also use this time to pray or talk to God, thanking Him for His blessings and seeking His purpose and direction in my life. This daily release of thoughts, feelings, and emotions is what keeps me out of my cell of "prison thinking."

After I have emptied myself, I need to refill the vacuum created. I read things that inspire and inform me. I read daily from the Bible, books of poetry, inspirational writings by various people, anything consistent with my values that inspires, informs, and motivates me to want to be a better person. Another key component of a daily quiet time is journaling. I have kept a daily journal for about ten years, not a diary but a journal. In this journal, I record anything inspirational or exhorting I read, hear, or come across. What are my thoughts, struggles I am having, relationships that need work, and how I am doing on my goals and objectives?

I frequently will revisit these journals and invariably am blessed by what I find and encouraged by how far I have come in whatever area I was struggling. Finally, my quiet time is when I can look at my personal compass and evaluate how I am doing. Am I living my core values? Maintaining my core purpose? Am I on course toward my vision? A quiet time is the main tool to navigate the twisting turns of my life.

I believe the main focus here is on simplicity of core purpose, core values, and vision, my personal compass. It is extremely easy for us to lose our focus and begin to drift off course, even seeking after "good things." The problem is that the good things become the enemy when they prevent us from doing the best things. There is always a balance and it is our personal compass that helps us stay on course.

My second stopping point is an accountability relationship with someone who loves me, knows my strengths and weakness, dreams and aspirations, and has the courage and boldness to tell me when I am not living what I say I am. My accountability partner is my wife, Lori, who I also happen to work with in our business. She is able to see me in action in virtually all situations, at my worst and at my best. She knows my core values, core purpose, and vision and does not hesitate in telling me when I am deviating from any of them.

When she irritates me the most is when I know she is the most right – sandpaper is abrasive, but it also removes the rough spots and makes them more receptive. The proverb that says, "As iron sharpens iron, so one man sharpens another" reminds me that when iron sharpens iron both heat and sparks are produced, but the net result is always a sharper and more usable instrument. My accountability partner keeps me sharp and helps complete me as a person.

My third stopping point is the accountability I feel when I am in fellowship with friends and family who share my core values and core purpose. One of the main places I get this is in my church, where I am constantly learning and being challenged by others to "raise the bar" on what I can accomplish. I also get this from my family, where I feel a special accountability to live with personal integrity and to be who I say I am. These are stopping points that work for me.

WHEN WE HIT A STOPPING POINT, WHAT DO WE DO?

We admit our mistakes, accept ourselves as imperfect, make amends if necessary, learn from the experience, pick ourselves up, and as Reagan said, "We move on with our life. This is the healthiest way to deal with a problem." When we are lost or off course, we return to our map and compass and begin to work the seven precepts of Navigating Change from precept number one, Positive Expectations. We should expect to fail; we are not perfect, and, in fact, it is the difficulties and the failures that give us the opportunities to grow.

THE VALUE OF ADVERSITY

A difficult world is positive for us. Overcoming one barrier gives us greater ability to overcome the next. If we look at great men and women of history, we will find the one common denominator to be their attitude toward adversity and perseverance in overcoming it.

Success is not measured by what a person has accomplished but what they have encountered and the courage with which they have struggled against overwhelming odds to overcome. It is only through testing and purifying ourselves in the hazards and pain of life that we grow. We must welcome the fact that life is a crucible and we will either emerge as a strong and useful band of purified steel or we will be spun off into the slag as worthless dross. Which way we go is not dependent upon our environment, opportunities, genetics, or background, it is dependent upon the choices we make.

We understand this principle so well in the physical world. For example, to choose to run a marathon race we know would take an extraordinary commitment, self-discipline, and lots of pain. As muscles needed to run this race are broken down during intense training, they grow back bigger and stronger, increasing our possibilities to run and finish the race. Pain makes gain is something we understand in the physical-conditioning realm.

But this principle applies equally to all components making up who we are: our mind, emotions, body, and spiritual life. We cannot disconnect these components and fully accomplish becoming the self-actualized person of purpose, passion, and peace we so desire. All these components are interdependent, and we must be healthy and balanced in all to become all we can become. This means taking the kind of healthy risks we talked of earlier, moving out of our "comfort zone" to claim "new territory": physically, intellectually, emotionally, and spiritually.

I like what Viktor Frankl said in Man's Search For Meaning: "God chooses what we go through, but we choose how we go through it." Every condition we encounter has hardships, hazards, and pains. We try to escape these conditions, delude ourselves, and make excuses and blame others for why they are happening to us when the only question over which we have any control is how will we choose to go through what is happening to us.

THE GREAT QUESTION

The great question is to what great purpose do we devote ourselves, what values do we hold so valuable as to be not negotiable, and what is our desired destination? This makes up our personal compass, and whether we follow it determines our responses to the circumstances of life; whether we will be strong in mind and heart or be weak and pitiable depends upon our use of the circumstances we are given.

During the Civil War, Union and Confederate forces met in what turned out to be the key battle of the entire war, The Battle of Gettysburg. General Lee and his Confederate Army had pushed into Pennsylvania in hopes of striking one last major blow to the Union, one that would turn public opinion against the war and bring it to an end, resulting in a divided country. Two huge armies met in a valley surrounded by low mountains overlooking the battlefield.

The high ground was critical and held by the Union Army. One particular low mountain, Little Round Top, was strategic for placement of artillery and was under the command of General Commander Joshua L. Chamberlain of the 20th Maine, Union Forces. Confederate forces stormed the mountain and there ensued the most important and bloody tactical encounter of the battle. Several assaults were repelled after close-quarter combat among warriors on both sides who just refused to give up.

Before the battle, Chamberlain, realizing the import of his position on Little Round Top Mountain, gave this speech to his men:

> *We know not of the future, and cannot plan for it much. But*
> *we can hold our spirits and bodies so pure and high, we may*
> *cherish such ideals, and dream such dreams of lofty purpose,*
> *that we can determine and know what manner of men we will*

be whenever and wherever the hour strikes that calls to noble
action...No man becomes suddenly different from his habit and
cherished thought.

I believe this is what life is all about. What will we do when we find
ourselves in this situation? Will we hold our spirits high and cherish
ideals of lofty dreams and noble purpose as Chamberlain said, and did,
or do we fold into a pitiable mass of quivering flesh, whining and
blaming others because the world doesn't give us what we want? The last
and only freedom we truly have is to choose which of these paths we will
follow.

The power and freedom in the words of Chamberlain are in his call to
"become" the right kind of person, one of values, purpose, and vision.
His point is that it is only through becoming this kind of person that we
are equipped and ready to meet the challenge of difficult circumstances
when they come.

HAVE A STOPPING POINT - KEY POINTS

- A stopping point is a feature beyond our designated destination that indicates to us we have missed our mark and are off course.

- Stopping points are typically time spent in a daily quiet time and accountability relationships with others.

- We are imperfect human beings. We will fall, stumble, and get off course.

- Overcoming one barrier gives us greater ability to overcome the next.

- The great question of life is to what great and noble purpose do we devote ourselves.

- When we hit a stopping point, we accept responsibility, forgive ourselves, make amends if necessary, and move on with our life.

KEY PRINCIPLES

- When we are lost or off course, we should return to our map and compass and begin to work the seven precepts of

Navigating Change. We should expect failure, we are not perfect, and, in fact, it is the difficulties and failures that give us the opportunity to learn and grow.

- Adversity is positive for us. If we look at all the great men and women of history, the one common denominator is their attitude toward adversity and their perseverance in overcoming it.

- As a knife is sharpened on a whetstone, so we are sharpened in our daily quiet time and our accountability relationships with others. Those who love us will be our toughest confronters.

KEY QUESTIONS

- How do you handle failure or rejection? Do you make excuses and wallow in self-pity or do you see it as an opportunity to learn and grow?

- Do you have a daily quiet time? If not then why not?

- Who is sharpening you? Keeping you from becoming a dull tool?

- Do you have trouble forgiving yourself and moving on?

SIMPLICITY

Never put happiness at center stage. It is the by-product of service, never the chief aim of life. Happiness is not a right to be grasped but a serendipity to be enjoyed.

- Richard Foster
Freedom of Simplicity

The secret to passion, peace, and purpose in our life is to live with detachment from material things and the opinions of other people. Living detached from things and people is what gives us the freedom to become all that we can become as individuals and organizations.

The opposite of detachment is attachment. Attachment is a dependence on things or people that give us the feeling they fill certain needs for personal significance or value. They enable us to feel needed and important and temporarily "warm and fuzzy." The feelings are based on false beliefs because they increase our dependence on them and thus, our desire to increase them. We can never be satisfied or at true peace with things. We simply spend our life seeking to add more and more, never feeling we have enough to be truly happy. Henry Ford, when asked what it would take to make him satisfied, said, "Just a little bit more."

This is not to say that material things and the opinions of others are not important, because they are. Attachment occurs when we cross the line of appreciation into obsession and dependence. Living a life of simplicity is not living the life of an ascetic but rather a life of independence and freedom from having to possess things. It is not the having of things that is wrong; it is the dependence upon having things that is wrong. It is all about the attitude we have.

I like the quote from Pope John the XXIII, who said, "The older I grow the more clearly I perceive the dignity and winning beauty of simplicity in thought, conduct, and speech: a desire to simplify all that is complicated and to treat everything with the greatest naturalness and clarity."

If simplicity is living a life without attachments or emotional dependence, what is it that holds us back? Fear holds us back, the kind of irrational or psychological fear that arises from separation from ourselves as well as others. Psychological fear is fear of the future, of what might happen. This kind of fear is different from reality fear, or fear of what we can see.

Psychological fear manifests itself in feelings that we will fail, be rejected, are not worthy, might be isolated, etc. It manifests itself in self-limiting beliefs like:

- We are powerless

- We are a victim of circumstances

- Life is too difficult

- We are unworthy

- Our condition seems hopeless

- We can't rely on others for help

- We are just the way we are. We can't change

- People won't like us if they really know us

- We might get hurt

- We don't deserve it

- We might have to change

It is these kind of self-limiting beliefs that cause us to want to be attached to something or someone. As long as we retain them, our life will be complex and difficult because we have given all our personal power and control over to things and other people. Simplicity begins with an understanding of our nature.

100% RESPONSIBILITY, COURAGE AND ACCEPTANCE

Once again, we have come back to the driving principle of life, 100% Responsibility. We are the problem, and nothing healthy will transpire in our growth toward the simple life until we come to grips with this reality.

Fear is a separating force intended to preserve our personal integrity, but, when we allow it to control us, it actually violates our personal integrity. Courage is what casts out fear. Courage is derived from the French word "coeur," which means heart. The "heart" means inner being or soul. When we talk of a person who has "heart," we mean that person possesses what it takes to do the right thing even though afraid. Courage is the opposite of fear, and where one dwells the other cannot.

Courage is what empowers us to give up fear of controlling and possessing things and people. It becomes the second step on the way to simplicity. The third step is acceptance. True acceptance is being able to accept the reality of our human need as being one of perpetual emptiness, of always seeking, but never really being fulfilled by material things and other people.

The pursuit of trying to "fill" this feeling of emptiness is what pushes us to seek attachments like possessions, money, or power -- anything to fill the vacuum. It is what makes life complex and creates anxiety. G. K. Chesterton said, "There are two ways to get enough: one is to continue to accumulate more and more. The other is to desire less."

This is not to say that material things are not good. However, there is a limit to good things, and, when that limit is exceeded, the good thing becomes the bad thing. The enemy of the best is the good. It takes 100% Responsibility, courage, and acceptance to know when this line has been crossed and to do something about it.

Simplicity is having the courage to take responsibility for oneself and accept the reality of our circumstances. It doesn't mean we have to be happy with them or to want to stay in them. It means we do not expend emotional and mental energy blaming others for why we are in the situation we are in. It means we and we alone take responsibility for what we can do and then we do it.

Whenever we experience difficulty in our lives, the very first thing we usually do is to look for someone to blame. We make excuses, whine, complain and expend enormous amounts of energy when the source of all this consternation resides not in the external circumstances but in our internal reaction to them. A life of blame and making excuses is not the simple life - it is the complicated life because we are continually off balance with things and people over which we have no real control.

ATTITUDE

The strife, turmoil, and chaos of the world are not what cause complexity, suffering, and unhappiness in our life. What causes these things is our inner attitude of heart and mind. We can choose our attitude in all circumstances. It is recognition of this and applying it to our life that creates simplicity. Life is very simple if we place it in this context. We can only control our own reactions to all situations.

FOCUS ON WHAT'S IMPORTANT!

Living a life of simplicity means maintaining focus on a few essential things, the enduring elements in our character: responsibility, integrity, faith, self-sacrifice, compassion, and service to others. It is out of these that flow the peace, purpose, and passion we seek, the need to be significant and be part of something bigger than ourselves.

A life of simplicity then is a life of self-leadership, of guiding that person we see in the mirror each morning. The irony is that if we focus our energy on directing that person we will find ourselves more and more outwardly focused on serving other people.

John Wooden, formerly the men's basketball coach at UCLA, is the most successful basketball coach in history. I believe he is the most successful coach ever, in any sport. My definition of success is not based on the number of victories he won but on the philosophy and character he was able to instill in the hundreds of players he coached.

Wooden's UCLA teams won seven consecutive NCAA championships and eleven titles in all, a record simply seen as unmatchable. I admire this man greatly and have studied his life, read his books, and, even though I have never met him, I feel I know him and trust him. What are his secrets to simplicity and success?

I believe the single most important factor in the success of Wooden was his attitude toward what he called preparation versus score. I call it process versus task. This is what he said:

THE SECRET TO SUCCESS

I had the greatest pride in how the players prepared, progressed, and performed. I felt this philosophy would have a much greater positive impact on the outcome of events than a stress on trying to outscore opponents. It's a focus on improving yourself rather than comparing yourself to the other team as indicated by the scoreboard. In fact, in thirty-one seasons of coaching I never once mentioned the word winning. I told them to keep their eyes off the scoreboard and instead focus on the fundamentals of shooting, passing, rebounding and team play, and to do it with the greatest passion and character. If they could walk off the court at the end of the game convinced they had done all these things they were winners regardless of what the scoreboard said.

When you get engrossed in those things over which you have no control, it will adversely affect those things over which you do have control, namely your preparation. You respect everyone.

Then you simply make the strongest effort to prepare to the fullest extent of your abilities. The result will take care of itself, and you should be willing to accept it.

Wooden also had simple values to align with and a guiding purpose that made up his personal compass. Here is what they were:

WOODEN'S VALUES: TWO SETS OF THREE

HONESTY

- Never Lie

- Never Cheat

- Never Steal

ADVERSITY

- Never Whine

- Never Complain

- Never Make Excuses

WOODEN'S SEVEN THINGS TO DO

- Be true to yourself

- Help others

- Make every day your masterpiece

- Drink deeply from good books, especially the Bible

- Make friendships a fine art

- Build a shelter of faith against a rainy day

- Pray for guidance and give daily thanks for your blessings

Simplicity, it seems to me, is bringing our core purpose and core values into a burning focus and aligning them with our actions as we trek through our lives. Alignment comes from living 100% Responsibility, acceptance of reality, and the courage to do something about it. This is, after all, the only thing we really have control over in our life.

I want to close with the Serenity Prayer because it draws into focus what it takes to live a simple and productive life: "Lord, grant me the serenity to accept those things I cannot change, the courage to change those I can change and the wisdom to know the difference."

SIMPLICITY - KEY POINTS

- Purpose, peace, and passion are the fruit of living a detached life free from dependence on material things and the opinions of others.

- Living a life of simplicity is not living the life of an ascetic but rather a life of independence and freedom from having to possess things. It is not the having of things that is wrong but rather the dependence on having things.

- Psychological fear hinders us from living a life of simplicity.

- 100% Responsibility, acceptance, clarity of purpose, and moral courage are the antidote for dependence and unhealthy thinking.

- Living a life of simplicity means bringing our core purpose, values, and vision into a burning focus and aligning our choices with them.

- A life of simplicity is one of self-leadership and directing that person we see in the mirror each morning.

KEY PRINCIPLES

- Nature abhors a vacuum. It is the pursuit of trying to fill a feeling of emptiness and lack of purpose that cause us to seek fulfillment in the possession of things and the opinions of others. These alternatives to real meaning and purpose simply make the problem worse and deaden us to the real issue.

- The strife, uncertainty, and chaos of the world are not what cause unhappiness in our life. What causes our unhappiness and lack of peace is our attitude toward the circumstances we find ourselves in.

- The process of living life is more important than accomplishments or completion of tasks. If we focus on the process of living our life with purpose and values then the accomplishments and task will take care of themselves.

KEY QUESTIONS

- Wooden said, "Focus on improving yourself rather than comparing yourself to the other team as indicated by the scoreboard." What did he mean by this?

LOVE AND THE LAW OF ATTRACTION

*To cheat oneself of love is the most terrible
deception; it is an eternal loss for which there
is no reparation, either in time or in eternity.*

\- Soren Kierkegaard

The highest need of humankind is to love others and be loved in return. Regardless of our efforts to hide, circumvent, or ignore this basic need, it drives our belief systems and ultimately our behavior. It is the pursuit of love that either fulfills or does not fulfill our personal sense of value and significance.

Hollywood and Madison Avenue are more aware of this basic human need than perhaps we are. The advertising world's understanding of the need for human acceptance and significance is what creates the illusion that, in order for us to be loved, we must look good, dress good, smell good, drive the right kind of car, eat the right kind of food, etc. They know that what we believe about these questions will drive our behavior and buying patterns.

The great irony is that love is so misunderstood. It has different meanings to different people, mostly driven by what the advertising media and Hollywood want us to believe. As a result, many of us have an entirely deluded perception of what love really is, what causes it, and where it comes from. We are told that it is how we feel, what our emotions are. When we are in love, birds sing, violins play, and our feet don't touch the ground.

THE PROBLEM WITH EMOTIONAL LOVE

The problem with emotional love, as Hollywood and Madison Avenue try to persuade us, is that it flies in the face of 100% Responsibility. Emotional love seems to say that we are controlled by outside factors and thus how we feel depends upon how others or our circumstances impact us. It follows that if we are dependent on others for love then we will be constantly buffeted to and fro at the whim of our circumstances and relationships. This is certainly our choice. We just need to be honest with ourselves about who or what is controlling our lives. It also follows that if we are dependent upon people and things for love then we also fall into the trap of needing to be needed by others, another form of dependency.

It is the pursuit of emotional love and its shallowness that produces the emotional pain in our lives we so much want to avoid. This presents the ultimate paradox of life: Our greatest need is also our greatest fear, and the harder we try to obtain it, the more difficult it is to obtain.

WHAT IS LOVE?

There are essentially three definitions under which the word "love" can be categorized. The first is **EMOTIONAL LOVE**. This kind of love is based on feelings generated by external circumstances and, therefore, tends to be transient and elusive. It can be characterized as: I'll love you if ... .

The second kind of love is **FRIENDSHIP LOVE**. This kind of love is derived from the Greek word "philadelphus," which means loving one's brother. This is the kind of love one might expect from a casual or close relationship with a friend or acquaintance. This would be a relationship based upon certain common interests or goals but not representing a deep commitment to one another. This kind of love can be characterized as: I'll love you because....

The third kind of love is **ACCEPTANCE** or **COMMITTED LOVE**. This kind of love is unconditional, unlike the other two kinds of love that depend upon conditional, external factors. Genuine acceptance is generated by an internal commitment to act in a certain way toward another person regardless of the actions of that person.

Genuine acceptance is a decision or choice we make to love another person not based upon their behavior but simply because we have made an internal commitment to ourselves to do so. This kind of love rests at the core of 100% Responsibility, which says that we always have a choice about our own reactions to any situation we find ourselves in. We cannot control our circumstances, but we can control and choose how we will respond to them. **COMMITTED LOVE IS A DECISION AND IS LEARNED, EXHIBITING ITSELF IN ACTIONS**. This kind of love can be characterized as: I love you ... period, no strings attached.

WHAT IS COMMITTED LOVE?

Commitment is a pledge and dedication to a long-term course of action. As this type of commitment is not conditional upon the other person, it places our personal integrity on the line. It is our internal commitment to self to carry out this action that determines its success or failure.

The greatest definition of this kind of love I have found is in I Corinthians 13: "If I speak in the tongues of men and of angels, but have not love, I am only a resounding gong or a clanging cymbal. If I have the gift of prophecy and can fathom all mysteries and all knowledge, and if I have a faith that can move mountains, but have not love, I am nothing. If I give all I possess to the poor and surrender my body to the flames, but have not love, I gain nothing." Love is:

- Patient

- Kind

- Does not envy others

- Is not arrogant or boastful

- Is not rude

- Is not self-seeking

- Is not easily angered

- Forgives and keeps no record of wrongs

- Delights not in evil

- Rejoices with the truth

- Always protects

- Always trusts

- Always hopes

- Always perseveres

- Love never fails

As I meditate on this great truth, I am struck with something profound indeed. There is nothing in this definition that tells me I must **feel** a certain way in order to love. The actions are all fairly easy to understand and are within my control and ability to carry out if I so choose. Neither are they dependent upon the other person responding in the way I want.

Committed love is not about feelings or emotions, as our culture will try to convince us, but rather is simply about doing the right thing and carrying out a pledge to do what we say regardless of the circumstances. This is the kind of love one might expect to experience toward God, spouse, or children.

WARNING

Acceptance or committed love does not mean commitment to accept all behavior but rather to accept the person. For example, we can love a child with unconditional love and still find certain behaviors totally unacceptable. The key to unconditional love is being able to separate who a person is from what they do, to be able to love one while not accepting the other. Consequently, genuine acceptance can be very tough indeed in terms of what it asks of another person. Real love can see the possibilities of others and long for their attainment.

WHY IS LOVE SO IMPORTANT?

A healthy understanding of love is critical to living our lives with purpose, passion, and peace. To love and be loved is the greatest need we have, one that drives everything we are and do. Love fulfills the greatest laws of nature and God. Jesus said that to love God and to love others is the fulfillment of the Law and satisfies all requirements of the Bible. I Corinthians 13 culminates by telling us that of faith, hope, and love, the greatest of all three is love. Why? Because to love fulfills the purpose and meaning for which we were all created.

We are human beings created for a purpose, and that purpose is to serve and love others and be loved in return. It is the being able to carry out this purpose that brings the sense of fulfillment we pursue so vigorously.

LOVE AND THE LAW OF THE HARVEST

It is also imperative that we understand the law of the harvest in this regard. We cannot give something to another that we do not possess. It would be insanity to believe we could love another without loving self first. We cannot give what we have not experienced and learned. But, if we have love, we can give it away freely because there is no fear that we will ever run out. It is like knowledge in that wise persons can teach all they want and still have the same knowledge they started with. We simply cannot give away all our genuine love. It is an internally generated and unlimited fount.

It is this universal love that enables us to fulfill the Gospel commandment to love our neighbors as we love ourselves. Soren Kierkegaard was a Danish philosopher and theologian who wrote the following on the subject of universal love: "It is, in fact, Christian love which discovers and knows that one's neighbor exists and that …it is one and the same thing …everyone is one's neighbor. If it were not a duty to love, then, there would be no concept of neighbor at all. But only when one loves his neighbor, only then is the selfishness of preferential love rooted out and the equality of the eternal preserved."

THREE THINGS THAT CAN KILL A RELATIONSHIP

- Selfishness

- Resentment

- Fear

All three of these characteristics can destroy a relationship. Selfishness is a totally inward focus without regard for the other person. Resentment is a crippling disease of the soul that steals personal responsibility from the holder and blames the other person. Fear makes us defensive, distant, and demanding, causing us to want to withdraw from the relationship.

AN ABUNDANCE ATTITUDE

It is human nature to self-protect and hoard out of a feeling of scarcity. There is only so much to go around so we cannot give up what we have. This is a false belief because growth and abundance come from sharing, serving, and giving away that which we have. The greatest paradox of life is that the more we try to hoard and protect, the less we will have. The more we give away, the more we receive.

Having an abundance attitude is what helps us to find win-win solutions where all parties benefit from the relationship. However, we must serve with the right motives, expecting nothing in return for what we give. When we do the right thing for the right motivation, it seems the outcome will also be right.

I like the following quote from Philippians 2: "Do nothing from selfishness or empty conceit, but with humility of mind let each of you regard one another as more important than himself; do not merely look out for your own personal interests but also for the interests of others."

THE LAW OF ATTRACTION

A basic tenet of interpersonal relationships is that like things attract. In other words, we tend to attract to ourselves that which we are. What is every man or woman but a magnet to attract or to be attracted? For instance, if we are angry, we will attract anger. Hate attracts hate, positive attracts positive, love attracts love, etc. Our beliefs produce our thinking, which produces our actions, which produces consequences, which reinforce the beliefs, and on and on we go.

We cannot attract those things that are different from the way we think. As James Allen says, "Every man's mind is like a fertile garden and whether he chooses to cultivate or not, that mind will bring forth whatever is allowed to grow there." Whatever we think is ultimately what we will produce. Thus, as surely as the sun rises, we attract those things of like quality to ourselves.

THE EIGHT-COW WIFE

I heard a story once about an African tribe whose ritual was to purchase their wives from fathers with a dowry that reflected the value of the woman. Value was typically defined as beauty, personality, skills, etc. Normally, the more beautiful the woman, the higher the dowry would be. If the woman had a good personality to go with her great looks, she might fetch as much as four cows. This would be an enormously high value.

One day a man from a different tribe visited in order to purchase a new wife. He was rich, handsome, and smart, thus all the women of the tribe who were eligible wanted to be his choice. Much to their surprise, he chose one of their members who was not only quite ordinary looking but also painfully shy. After making his decision, he announced to the astounded father that she was worth eight cows.

News of the inflated value spread throughout the village, and people were shocked and dismayed. The man soon left with his new wife, taking her to his own village. One year later, the couple returned to the woman's village to visit, and the people gathered to welcome them. As the tribe gathered about the couple, they became aware of the radical change that had occurred in the woman. She had become quite beautiful, vivacious, and bubbling with personality.

The villagers, being curious about how this could have happened, queried the man. His reply to their questions was that he had simply chosen to see her possibilities and made a decision to treat her as if she were an eight-cow wife instead of a four-cow wife. This simple decision attracted to her those qualities he desired her to have. She had become what he was able to see her becoming and not what she was.

The law of attraction is consistent with the law of love and what the golden rule teaches about doing unto others. We will attract to ourselves those characteristics that we are and what we desire to see in others. If we, therefore, desire to be a person of purpose, peace, and passion then that is what we must become. If we desire to see love in others, then we must love, just as the villager did with his wife. It is our choice to love or not love, to hate or not hate, and the choice we make will determine what we will ultimately become. **WE ARE THEN WHAT WE CHOOSE TO BECOME, AND WE ATTRACT TO OURSELVES THAT WHICH WE CHOOSE TO ATTRACT.**

Only we can change ourselves. We should not expect our parents, family, friends, or profession to change us. We can alter any aspect of our life once we accept that we are the product of our decisions. Continue to do what we have always done before and the results will remain the same. Revamp our approach to life and we will produce a different outcome.

This is certainly true of the greatest need of humankind: to love and be loved. Love is a choice, a decision in our lives that involves a commitment to another person or persons to honor, value, and respect them. The paradox is that the more love we give away to others the more we will attract to ourselves, thereby meeting our own greatest need. We attract that which we are and give away to others.

LOVE AND THE LAW OF ATTRACTION - KEY POINTS

- The highest need of humankind is to love others and be loved in return.

- The great irony is that love is so misunderstood.

- Emotional love, as Hollywood and Madison Avenue present it, flies in the face of 100% Responsibility.

- Emotional love seems to say we are controlled by outside factors, beyond our control.

- There are three categories of love: emotional, friendship, and committed.

- Committed love is an unconditional choice to honor and respect another person regardless of their actions toward us. It is being able to separate who a person is from what they do. We can love one and hate the other.

- Commitment is a pledge to oneself to a long-term course of action. It places our personal integrity on the line, as it is our internal commitment to self that determines its success or failure.

KEY PRINCIPLES

• Committed love is a decision, is learned, and is exhibited
through our actions.

• Human nature is to self-protect out of a feeling of scarcity.
Growth and abundance come from sharing, serving, and giving
away that which we have. The greatest paradox of life is that
the more we try to hoard and protect, the less we will have.
The more we give away, the more we receive.

• We tend to attract that which we are. We are like a magnet for
our own attitude: love attracts love, hate attracts hate,
negativism attracts negativism, etc. We cannot attract those
things different than we think and subsequently act.

KEY QUESTIONS

• James Allen said, "Every man's mind is like a fertile garden
and whether he chooses to cultivate or not, that mind will bring
forth whatever is allowed to grow there." What does he mean
by this?

CONTINUAL GROWTH

Renew thyself completely each day; do it again, and again, and forever again. The morning, which is the most memorable season of the day, is the awakening hour. Then there is some part of us, which awakes for this hour and then slumbers all the rest of the day and night. All memorable events, I should say, transpire in morning and in a morning atmosphere.

- Henry David Thoreau

I have touched on the subject of continual growth throughout this book, and it is, in fact, a general theme. I do, however, want to emphasize the import of having an attitude of continual growth by devoting a chapter to it. I personally hold this value so high as to make it one of my core values.

What is continual growth? First, it is an attitude; an attitude that we will forever and continuously seek to grow, mature, make better decisions, and simply live our life better. It is a commitment to self to become healthier in our physical, spiritual, emotional, and intellectual lives. It is also recognizing the reality that we are neither perfect nor will we ever be so, but this should not prevent us from **seeking** to be perfect in everything we do.

WARNING

While seeking to perfect oneself is a virtue, crossing the line into dependence upon being perfect is unhealthy. Perfectionism, or dependence upon being perfect, is not a healthy attitude and can lead us into all manner of unhealthy behaviors. A healthy attitude would be one where we seek to be perfect while recognizing the reality we will never be so. It is continually striving toward becoming a better person in all aspects of our lives while not being imbalanced or dependent on any of them.

LIVING A BLAMELESS LIFE

Perfectionism is antithetical to blamelessness. Perfectionism is a **dependence** upon being perfect in order to esteem and value self. Since we are not perfect, we develop all kinds of devious strategies and delusions to circumvent dealing with the reality of who we are.

Living a blameless life, however, is the opposite, in that, while striving to be perfect, we accept the reality that we are not and never will be on this earth. We are able to accept and to forgive ourselves for our shortcomings and move on with our life, learning how to do it better next time. A blameless life means we never make excuses, blame, or rationalize why we failed or fell back from our ideals or goals. We accept responsibility for the fact we messed up, forgive ourselves, and others if appropriate, and move on to correct the problem and do it better. In this attitude, we become the solution rather than continuing to be the problem.

Living a blameless and excellent life is based upon achieving a balance between logic and emotions. This can only be accomplished by discernment of life on all levels of who we are: physically, spiritually, emotionally, and intellectually. It is only when we are balanced and blameless that we are capable of noble and productive interdependent relationships with others. Thus all maturity and personal growth comes back to leading that person we see in the mirror each morning.

THE VALUE OF SOLITUDE

The secret to living a life of continual growth is reserving, as a priority, time alone in solitude. Solitude is a state of attitude, not a place. An attitude of solitude neither fears being alone nor fears being with others. It is a place of balance where we feel secure in ourselves and in alignment with our core purpose, values, and vision. We are not controlled by circumstances or others but rather our personal compass. I like the quote by Dietrich Bonhoeffer on this subject:

> *Let him who cannot be alone beware of community. Let him who is not in community beware of being alone. Each by itself has profound perils and pitfalls. One who wants fellowship without solitude plunges into the void of words and feelings, and one who seeks solitude without fellowship perishes in the abyss of*

vanity, self-infatuation, and despair.

What Bonhoeffer is saying is that we must cultivate as part of our maturity and growth both the stillness of solitude and the community of meaningful relationships with others if we want to live a balanced and productive life. Solitude is both a combination of lack of speech and listening. Listening for what? Listening for the reality of who we are and what is going on in our life. It is this reality that produces change. Remember people do not change until the pain of not changing is greater than the pain of changing.

We must listen daily and, as Thoreau said, the early morning is "the most memorable season of the day." An early morning quiet time is the most important gift I can give myself, for it is a time when I can examine my thoughts, emotions, behaviors, and myself. It is a time when I can seek to align myself with my personal compass. There is nothing more important in my life than quiet time where I may meditate, pray, and refocus on what is most important in my life. The fruit of this time is a better relationship with God, others, and myself.

CONTINUAL LEARNING

The goal of every person or team should be to develop sustainable growth and learning. A learning person will be a growing person. It is fairly easy to learn during a crisis because we have no choice. We either learn or we fail. It is much more difficult to sustain continual growth and learn to think in new and creative ways when there is no compelling reason to do so. As in everything else we have discussed, it all begins in our attitude or the way we think.

Learn to see life as an adventure, a journey into becoming a more whole, integrated, and balanced person. Living life as an adventure implies our willingness to take healthy risk and not sit in a self-protected, defensive stance. To learn is to continually challenge ourselves to expand our comfort zone by pushing into untamed territory. Growth also requires us to unlearn as well as learn.

PERSONAL LIFE CHOICES

Self-awareness, consciousness, and self-realization all must precede choice. Thus the most important decision we will make in life is that of gripping the reality of who we really are, not what we wish we were. This does not make our choices less difficult. In fact, they make our decisions more difficult by multiplying our options.

Anger is an example. Anger is a blocked goal and is generated when someone or something interferes with our conscious or subconscious objectives. For instance, if someone communicates dishonor by interrupting us, the initial emotion might be anger because our goal of expressing self has been blocked. It is easy for us to either respond in assertive anger over the slight or to be passively angry and withdraw from the conversation or relationship. Either response is unhealthy.

If we are to grow in the process of handling our emotions, we must first understand the reality of what is happening to us. Expressing anger in either a hostile or passive manner is giving up control of self to the person we are angry toward. The next step in the process is to acknowledge the emotion and accept 100% Responsibility for how we are going to respond to it.

Processing the why of our anger will probably lead us to a false belief, such as the belief that we need the approval of this person in order to have value. The fact is, we do not need the approval of this or any other person. It is acknowledging this and changing the way we think that causes us to change our reaction to it. By being willing to acknowledge, accept, and take responsibility for our reaction, we are able to grow. This example illustrates the power of 100% Responsibility as the foundation for change and growth. It is indeed liberating to realize that we can change our behavior by changing the way we think.

THE ALTERNATIVE

The alternative is to not confront the problem, to live in denial and blame, never venturing from our comfort zone. Most of us prefer to live in this zone of comfort and never venture into the untamed realm of uncertainty and insecurity. The problem with living our life in the comfort zone is that we remain stale and our thinking reinforced with a negative view of how to relate to the problems of life. It is a slow, agonizing emotional and spiritual death. Real growth requires healthy risk, pain, and discomfort, but the payoff is purpose, passion, and peace.

I like the quote by M. Scott Peck, M.D., on this subject: "The only real security in life lies in relishing life's insecurities."

Henry David Thoreau also addressed the principle of continual growth in this quote:

> *I went to the woods because I wished to live deliberately, to front only the essential facts of life, and see if I could not learn what it had to teach, and not when I came to die, discover that I had not lived. I did not wish to practice resignation, unless it was quite necessary. I wanted to live deep and suck out all the marrow of life so sturdily and Spartan-like as to put to rout all that was not life.*

Thoreau is talking about the boredom, staleness, and lack of vitality that exist in the comfort zone of life. It is a place without zest where we simply exist and agree with self to grow no more. After spending his two years at Walden Pond, Thoreau wrote this:

I left the woods for as good a reason as I went there. Perhaps it seemed to me that I had several more lives to live, and could not spare any more time for that one ... I learned this, at least, by my experiment; that if one advances confidently in the direction of his dreams, and endeavors to live the life which he has imagined, he will meet with a success unexpected in common hours.

FREEDOM AND TRUTH

People who have freed themselves from denial and illusions, who have seen through the game of life with all its love and hate, joys and sorrow, success and failure, have come to realize that life is inherently unpredictable, difficult, and unfair. Most of us, however, live in a state of denial about various issues, out of touch with reality and bound in slavery to one thing or another.

The only solution to this problem, endemic in humankind, is to seek and find a higher truth. The highest truth of life must be sought spiritually and not intellectually, although the totality of our being requires us to maintain a healthy balance between our physical, spiritual, intellectual, and emotional lives.

The search for truth and wisdom is not one that will ever be taken by the mass of people but rather by a few who walk or seek to walk through that narrow door. Freedom comes from giving up and disassociating our self from the notion that life is fair. Life is not fair! To search for and depend upon the idea that life is fair is to live in bondage.

But those few who step to the forefront take 100% Responsibility for how they respond to the vagaries of life will influence and guide not only themselves but others as well. We must learn that we cannot command things and can only command self. We can only mold and master our own will and cannot coerce or command the will of others. It is in being the right person that we have freedom.

CONTINUAL GROWTH - KEY POINTS

- Continual growth is an attitude that we will forever and continuously seek to grow, mature, make better decisions, and live our life better.

- While seeking perfection is a virtue, crossing the line into dependence on being perfect is not healthy. Perfectionism is a destructive and unhealthy behavior.

- Living a blameless life is antithetical to perfectionism. A blameless life accepts our human imperfections and allows us to forgive ourselves and move on.

- Solitude is not a place but a state of attitude and is what enables us to examine ourselves with clarity of purpose, learn, and grow.

- A learning person is a growing person. Learning implies gaining knowledge and truth and using it to change our behavior. New action is what proves to us that we have learned something new.

- It is more difficult to learn in times where there is a lack of crisis as there is no compelling reason to do so.

KEY PRINCIPLES

• Self-awareness must precede choice. The most important decision we will make in life is that of gripping the reality of who we really are, not what we wish we were.

• Continual growth requires that we live on the healthy edge of our comfort zone, ready to leap into the untamed territory. It is this continual leap that gives us the new experience to process and learn from.

KEY QUESTIONS

• M. Scott Peck said, "The only real security in life lies in relishing life's insecurities." What did he mean by this?

• Do you agree that we must continually take healthy risk, leaping into the unknown territory in order to grow and mature?

• Where are you living? On the edge or safely back from the edge?

THE TESTED METAL

The first responsibility of a leader is to define reality. The last is to say thank you. In between, the leader is a servant.

- Max DePree

We define leadership at Team Trek as KNOWING THE DIRECTION IN WHICH YOU DESIRE TO TRAVEL AND INFLUENCING OTHERS TO FOLLOW. I believe this is exactly what Max DePree is saying in the above quote: reality consists of core values, core purpose, and vision combined with clarity of available resources and capabilities.

Leadership of others is not possible without leadership of self. We must first lead that person we see in the mirror each morning and become trustworthy persons of character and competence. Becoming trustworthy is within the scope of our abilities if we choose to live our lives with 100% Responsibility and develop and use a compass to guide us in our journey. The first thirteen chapters of this field book have been devoted to learning to lead self.

This final chapter will address the new and improved product: a sharpened blade of strong and burnished steel forged in the crucible of life. We are ready to serve, teach, coach, mentor, and encourage others to become all they can. Leaders secure with themselves are available to give themselves away to others, and this becomes one of the greatest paradoxes of life: the more we give away, the more we receive. One of my favorite quotes on leadership is by Admiral James B. Stocksdale:

> *Leadership must be based on goodwill.... It means obvious and wholehearted commitment to helping followers ... What we need for leaders are men and women of heart who are so helpful that they, in effect, do away with need of their jobs. But leaders like that are never out of a job, never out of followers. Strange as it sounds, great leaders gain authority by giving it away.*

OUR DIFFERENCES

People are influenced for their reasons, not our reasons, and these have to do with basic needs they desire to have met. We all have different personality traits, preferences, talents, experiences, and perspectives. This is what creates a rich opportunity for a group of diverse people to produce something greater as a group than they can produce individually. This is synergy, when two opposites can combine to produce something greater than either could produce alone. This is exactly what happens in medicine when two opposing drugs may interact to produce a desired effect that neither could produce by itself. In other words, one plus one can potentially equal three or more.

OUR SAMENESS

The key to synergy is not recognition of the differences we have but recognition of our sameness. Despite our differences, we are motivated to commitment by the meeting of the same basic needs. These needs are:

- The need for acceptance, to love and be loved.

- The need to be understood.

- The need for significance, importance, contribution, and value.

MOTIVATIONAL THEORY

According to Abraham Maslow's theory on motivation, behavior is triggered by a need deficit driving the individual to reduce the tension it creates. Tension leads to behavior that will potentially satisfy the need. The above stated needs are what he calls the higher needs in the hierarchy of needs. If you accept this theory then commitment from a follower will only emanate from meeting the need to be accepted, understood, and significant. In other words, when a person feels needed and involved in a noble and higher purpose, they will commit; if they do not, they will not.

There are other lower needs in the Maslow hierarchy such as safety needs, social needs, and physiological needs such as food, water, etc. Money and other monetary compensation fall into the lower category.

What he is saying is we can get a person's mind and hands through satisfying lower hierarchical needs, but the heart can only be captured through meeting the highest needs. I believe real leadership is of the heart, and a leader who influences others to follow with head, heart, and hands is that leader who will attain real success.

LEADING FROM THE HEART

How do we do this? How do we know what it takes to generate commitment from those we desire to influence? Part of our teambuilding program at Team Trek involves using a model where we ask participants to create a picture of a person they would be willing to follow with head, heart, and hands. A person they would commit to follow with passion, purpose, and enthusiasm. Every group creates exactly the same model, whether they are a corporate executive group or an eighth-grade class.

We have validated this with hundreds of groups, and the consistency is simply amazing. This model validates the kind of person we need to become if we desire to become a leader of influence, capturing the heart of those we desire to lead. Following is a compilation of what that person looks like:

- Communicates purpose, values, and possibilities for the organization and for me.

- Empathic listener.

- Positive and enthusiastic.

- Does not blame or make excuses.

- Acts with integrity in all things.

- Encourages, coaches, and mentors. Has a servant attitude.

- Challenges the status quo.

- Sense of humor; celebrates victories.

- Empowers, enables me to act, and holds me accountable.

- Authentic and approachable.

There is a common denominator that runs through most of these traits. This person influences us not because they are great but because they make us want to be great. We feel significant, understood, and accepted around this person. **This person, by caring about us, makes us care about what they have to say. We feel involved in the process and, therefore, committed to it.** This is not my model, nor is it the Team Trek model. It's what thousands of people have simply told us would be required in order for them to give it all.

There are two other important points to learn from this exercise:

- The leadership traits are all acquired skills, not ones we are born with.

- The traits are exactly the same for an effective follower as they are for someone we would follow.

Thus what has been created is not the perfect leader model but rather the perfect leader/follower model. In a healthy, functioning organization, leadership will tend to shift among the group based upon the power of an idea, situation, experience, and ability to influence others. Leadership is not a title under this definition, and everyone is capable of being both an effective leader and effective follower depending upon the situation and circumstances. This is what true situational leadership is all about. We become that which best influences and facilitates the purpose and goals of the organization of which we are a part.

What hinders us from becoming this person? If we are honest, we will admit it is only self that hinders us. Excuses, blaming, and justifying are what hinder us. Prison thinking is what hinders us. It always comes back to leading ourselves and living our life with 100% Responsibility, seeing ourselves as the problem and the solution and doing something about it. People yearn for an effective leader, one that will influence them to want to be great.

There is a Chinese proverb on leadership I like:

A bad leader makes you feel bad about yourself. A good leader makes you feel good about him or her. A great leader makes you feel great about yourself.

THE EAGLE

The eagle thrives in altitudes and seems to long for the storm because those thermal updrafts of the storm cause her to soar higher than she could without the storm. The storm is no longer a threat to her because she spreads her powerful wings and glides above the ink-black clouds below.

Initially, the storm compels her to fly faster, farther, and higher. Whereas her normal speed might be fifty miles an hour, she may be clocked as fast as one hundred miles an hour during a storm. Those turbulent winds that would knock most birds from the sky, defeating them in the process, only cause the eagle to reach its greatest potential. All of us will be buffeted by these kinds of life storms. Some of us will want to give up. It is too much for us. But, like the eagle, we can soar above it all, reaching great heights, realizing our possibilities, and living a life of purpose, passion, and peace, if only we choose to do so. We can use adversity to both survive and thrive.

CONCLUSION

Solomon, circa 935 B.C., King of Israel, is recognized as one of the wisest and richest men who ever lived. He is generally thought of as the author of the books The Song of Songs, Proverbs, and Ecclesiastes in the Old Testament of the Bible. His struggle to live his life amid bountiful material things and to find meaning and purpose mirrors the trek of many of us through life.

The book of Ecclesiastes, in particular, is the crying out of a man searching for the meaning of life and willing to try almost anything to discover it. His plaintive cry is heard in chapter two:

I denied myself nothing my eyes desired;
I refused my heart no pleasure.
My heart took delight in all my work,
And this was the reward for all my labor.
Yet when I surveyed all that my hands had done,
And what I had toiled to achieve,
Everything was meaningless, a chasing after the wind;
Nothing was gained under the sun.

Then I turned my thoughts to wisdom and found it better than folly,

But I came to realize that the same fate overtakes them both.

Then I thought in my heart, the fate of the fool will overtake me also.

What then do I gain by being wise?

I said in my heart,

"This too is meaningless."

For the wise man, like the fool, will not be long remembered;

In days to come both will be forgotten.

Like the fool, the wise man will die also.

These words from a man who was wise, handsome, rich, and blessed in all ways should haunt us as we think about our own journey through life. Solomon, after agonizing about the ultimate meaning of life finally, concludes in the final chapter that his purpose is to live in obedience to God, knowing that in the end all things will be judged as to their good or evil.

DISCOVER PURPOSE AND LIVE IT

The meaning of life lies in discovering our individual purpose and living it. This purpose will ultimately be whatever we leave behind in wlife we have created that money cannot buy and death cannot take away. In the end all our baubles, titles, and trophies will be in a garage sale somewhere or distributed to someone who within a short time will not remember where they came from. The only legacy we will leave behind is the impact we have had on other people. How are others living out what they learned by watching us live our lives? I want to repeat a quote from George Bernard Shaw that I used earlier in the book. It is one of my all-time favorites:

This is the true joy in life, being used for a purpose recognized as a mighty one ... being a force of nature instead of a feverish, selfish little clod of ailments and grievances, complaining that the world will not devote itself to making you happy.

This quote by Shaw says it all. "Find our noble purpose or task in life and live it without making excuses, whining, or blaming others for why we can't carry it out."

This is 100% Responsibility and in the end is what life is all about.

Our life has a beginning, middle, and an end. I believe our greatest fear is not so much when that end comes as the fear of not ever having lived at all. It is not the prospect of death that frightens most of us. It is we will never have made a difference, never been significant, never loved or been loved. As Thoreau said, "That we would have died without ever having lived at all."

In Mark Twain's novel *Tom Sawyer*, there is a scene in which Tom and Huck return after having "run away from home." Upon returning, they find, to their surprise, all their friends and family gathered at the church conducting Tom's funeral.

As Tom listens to his own funeral from the church attic, he hears the eulogies of people who believe he has died. The town's people recount Tom with great fondness, and he is able to see what a difference he made in the lives of others during his short life.

Isn't this, in the final analysis, all that we will leave behind? The impact we had on the lives of others, the parachutes we packed, the difference we made in the world because we simply lived.

If we had the opportunity to attend our own memorial service, as Tom Sawyer did, what would we want people to say about the difference we made in their lives? Our family, friends, associates, and others who have passed through our life would have an opportunity to testify. What would we want them to say?

I want to conclude this book with a story. In the l960s, Leonard Bernstein, a conductor and composer, wrote a musical tribute to then-President John F. Kennedy. The tribute, called *Mass*, was about the life of a priest who rose from modest beginnings to a position of great influence, wealth, and power.

In the final scene of the tribute, the priest is seen standing on stage dressed in incredible liturgical robes. On his feet are slippers made with pure gold thread. On his head is a gold crown, sparkling with diamonds in the stage lights. Around his neck is a gold cross containing rubies and sapphires and upon his fingers are rings of every configuration. The priest holds in his arms a beautiful crystal chalice and a staff encrusted with jewels.

Also on stage are a number of people dressed in normal, everyday clothing. Suddenly, the people approach the priest and lift him upon their shoulders and begin marching around the stage singing praises to his name. After several minutes, just as suddenly, the adoring crowd drops the priest to the floor.

As the priest hits the stage the beautiful crystal chalice flies from his arms and shatters into a thousand pieces. The crowd then leaps upon the priest and tears from him his robes, crown, staff, rings, and jewels. They depart, taking it all with them. The priest now stands forlornly in the middle of the stage, having had everything that defined who he was   suddenly stripped away. The material things, the power and influence over others, suddenly and unexpectedly gone. He now stands, in a pair of cut-off jean shorts, amid a pile of broken glass, alone.

He stands for what seems like forever, his head hung, gazing at the broken glass at his feet. He slowly ponders what has happened, undoubtedly reflecting on the unfairness of it all and wondering how this could have happened to him. After a period of wallowing in self-pity over his plight, he slowly reaches down and picks up a piece of the broken glass and holds it up to the light.

As he rotates the broken glass in his fingers, he notices a beautiful prism of color caused by the stage lights hitting the glass and fracturing. Intrigued, he rotates the glass again with the same result, another beautiful prism of colors. He turns it again with a similar result. He continues to turn the glass as a smile slowly comes over his face and he utters the final words of the play: "I never realized that broken glass could be so beautiful."

Now here is the picture. The priest represents us, and the chalice is our life. It wasn't until the chalice was broken that it could really produce real beauty and service to others. Before it was broken, it was simply a piece of crystal to gaze upon though having no real purpose. After it was broken, it could produce color, light, and value. This is our purpose: to be broken, humble, and available to serve others and help them become what they can become. It is through this process that we become all we can become. The reward is being able to live with the purpose, peace, and passion we so desire.

THE TESTED METAL - KEY POINTS

- The definition of leadership is to know the direction in which we desire to travel and influence others to follow.

- Leadership of others is not possible without leadership of self.

- People are influenced for their reasons, not our reasons.

- People do not care what we know until they know that we care.

- The richness of our **differences** can only be effectively utilized when we understand and motivate one another from our **sameness**.

- A leader who could influence us to follow with head, heart, and hands is one who makes us want to be better. Someone who can see and communicate our possibilities.

- We hinder only ourselves in becoming the perfect leader/ follower.

- Effective leaders influence others to want to be great.

KEY PRINCIPLES

- The meaning of life is discovering our life purpose and living it. This purpose will ultimately be whatever we leave behind in life that money cannot buy and death cannot take away.

- Find our noble purpose in life and then live it without making excuses, whining, or blaming others for why we can't carry it out. This is 100% Responsibility and in the end is what life is all about.

KEY QUESTIONS

- If you could project yourself to your own memorial service and you had the opportunity of attending, as an unseen observer, what would you want those giving testimonies to say about the impact you had on their lives? Do you agree that this is the only real legacy you will leave, the impact you have had on the lives of others?

LEFT OVER NUGGETS FROM THE CRUCIBLE

There are red letter days in our lives when we meet people who thrill us like a fine poem, people whose handshake is a brimful of unspoken sympathy and whose sweet, rich nature imparts to our eager impatient spirits a wonderful restfulness ... perhaps we never saw them before and they may never cross our life's path again; but the influence of their calm, mellow nature is a libation poured out upon our discontent, and we feel its healing touch as the ocean feels the mountain stream freshening its brine ...

-Helen Keller

Your self image should not come from your job but how well you do your job. Even if your job is sweeping streets you have to sweep them as good as Leonardo da Vinci painted or Beethoven wrote music.

-Dr. Martin Luther King

Most anyone can stand adversity, but to test a person's character, give him power.

-Abraham Lincoln

Of all the virtues we can learn, no trait is more useful, more essential for survival and more likely to improve the quality of life than the ability to transform adversity into an enjoyable challenge.

-Mihalyi Csikszentmihaly

I took stock of myself and set aside my pouting and excuse-making. I decided that I loved the game so much that I would devote all my energies to being the best I could be. I wasn't going to blame anybody for keeping me from becoming what I knew I could become.

-Mark McGuire
St. Louis Cardinals First Baseman
(on how he overcame the worst
slump of his career in 1991)

The best people foster the good in others, not the bad. The worst people foster the bad in others, not the good.

-Confucius

Life is too short to waste in critic peep or cynic bark; quarrel or reprimand: Twill soon be dark; Up! Mind thine own aim, and God speed the mark!

-Ralph Waldo Emerson

There is no sin punished more implacably by nature than the sin of resistance to change.

-Ann Morrow Lindbergh

Be sure you know the condition of your flocks, give careful attention to your herds: for riches do not endure forever, and a crown is not secure for all generations.

-Proverbs 27:23

If you treat an individual as he is, he will stay as he is. But if you treat him as if he were what he ought to be and could be he will become what he ought to be, and what he could be.

-Goethe

The purest treasure mortal times afford is—spotless reputation: that away, men are but guilded loam, or painted clay.

-William Shakespeare

Two things seemed pretty apparent to me. One was, that in order to be a Mississippi River pilot a man has got to learn more than any man ought to be allowed to know; and the other was, that he must learn it all over again in a different way every twenty-four hours.

-Mark Twain

Meditation has no point or no reality unless it is firmly rooted in life.

-Thomas Merton

The real benefactors of mankind are the men and women who can raise their fellow beings out of the world of coin and money; who make them forget their bank account by interesting them in their higher selves; who can raise mere money-getters into the intellectual realm, where they will cease to measure greatness and happiness by dollars and cents; who can make men forget their stomachs and feast on beings banquet.

-Ralph Waldo Emerson

True Godliness does not turn men out of the world, but enables them to live better in it and excites their endeavors to mend it.

-William Penn

Let him who cannot be alone beware of community. Let him who is not in community beware of being alone. Each by itself has profound perils and pitfalls. One who wants fellowship without solitude plunges into the void of words and feelings, and one who seeks solitude without fellowship perishes in the abyss of vanity, self-infatuation, and despair.

-Dietrich Bonhoeffer

A man is rich in proportion to the number of things which he can afford to let alone.

-Henry David Thoreau

THE ART OF STRATEGY

Those who are victorious plan effectively and change decisively. They are like a great river that maintains its course but adjusts its flow ... they have form but are formless. They are skilled in both planning and adapting and need not fear the results of a thousand battles; for they win in advance, defeating those that have already lost.

-Sun-tzu
Chinese Warrior/Philosopher

Why stand we here idle? What is it that gentlemen wish? What would they have? Is life so dear, or peace so sweet, as to be purchased at the price of chains and slavery? Forbid it, Almighty God! I know not what course others may take; but as for me, give me liberty, or give me death.

-Patrick Henry, March 23, 1775
Speech to Virginia House of Burgesses

We can in no way assist our enemies more effectually than by making division among ourselves.

-General George Washington, 1776

Do not take counsel of your fears.

-General Thomas "Stonewall" Jackson

PROVERBS ON LEADERSHIP

• *A good leader motivates, doesn't mislead, doesn't exploit.*

- *A good leader abhors wrongdoing of all kinds; sound leadership has a moral foundation.*
- *A good leader cultivates honest speech; they love advisors who tell them the truth.*
- *An intemperate leader wreaks havoc in lives; you are smart to stay clear of someone like that.*
- *Good-tempered leaders invigorate lives; they are like spring rain and sunshine.*
- *We don't expect eloquence from fools, nor do we expect lies from our leaders.*
- *Wise men and women are always learning, always listening for fresh ideas.*
- *Mean-tempered leaders are like mad dogs; the good-natured are like fresh morning dew.*
- *Ignorant zeal is worthless.*
- *After careful scrutiny, a wise leader makes a clean sweep of rebels and dolts.*
- *Do your best, prepare for the worst and then trust God to bring you victory.*
- *As iron sharpens iron so one friend sharpens another.*
- *When a leader listens to malicious gossip, all the workers get infected.*
- *A leader of good judgment gives stability; an exploiting leader leaves a trail of waste.*
- *When the country is in chaos everyone has a plan to fix it. But it takes a leader of real understanding to straighten things out.*
- *He one who knows much says little; an understanding person remains calm.*

In our country, most any fool can be a success at something. The problem with success is that it leads to failure. When you are on top there is no place to go but down ... Success is how high you can bounce when you hit bottom.

-General George Patton

For it is as difficult to make a people free that is resolved to live in servitude as it is to subject a people to servitude that is determined to be free.

-Niccolo Machiavelli

Make a tree good and its fruit will be good, or make a tree bad and its fruit will be bad, for a tree is recognized by its fruit.

-Matthew 12:34

There is no security on this earth; only opportunity.

-General Douglas MacArthur

HOW ORGANIZATIONS CRUMBLE AND FALL

The Romans were secure of their liberty, and did not see any enemies who could frighten them. This security and the weakness of their enemies induced the Romans to name Consuls, not on the basis of virtue, but of popularity, elevating to those office men who knew how to charm the people, not those who knew how to defeat their enemies; then later, from those most charming they descended to those most powerful, so that the good men ... were completely excluded.

-Niccolo Machiavelli

FORMULA FOR A BALANCED LIFE

Do not be over righteous, nor be over wise.
Do not be over wicked,
And do not be a fool,
Why die before your time?
t is a good thing to grasp the one
And not let go of the other.
The man who loves God
Will avoid all extremes.

- Ecclesiastes 7:15-18

Shall we whine and cry for relief, and see one province after another fall to despotism? The line ought to be drawn. The crisis is arrived when we must assert our rights.

-General George Washington

The American cause will either be won through perseverance and fortitude, or lost through cowardice and submission.

-Thomas Paine, 1776

CREED OF THE OPEN ROAD

- *To live our highest*
- *To aid in righting wrongs*
- *To keep our faces to the light*
- *To love all creatures*
- *To do our own thinking*
- *To do our duty*
- *To remain humble and strong*

- *To not judge others*
- *To get up when we stumble*
- *To fear nothing, except our own wrongdoing*
- *To recognize the good in all people*
- *To avoid excess*
- *To know that work is an established condition of happiness*
- *Thoughts are forces*
- *To be honest, fearless, just, joyous, and kind*

-Ralph Waldo Trine

Do not be too moral. You may cheat yourself out of much life so. Aim above morality. Be not simply good; be good for something.

-Henry David Thoreau

Let all be harmonious, sympathetic, brotherly, kindhearted, and humble in spirit; not returning evil for evil, or insult for insult, but giving a blessing instead; for you were called for the very purpose that you might inherit a blessing.

-1 Peter 3:8-10

We have to understand that the world can only be grasped by action, not by contemplation .... The most powerful drive in the ascent of a man (woman) is his pleasure in his own skill. He loves to do what he does well and, having done it well he loves to do it better

-Jacob Bronowski

If you want happiness for an hour - take a nap.
If you want happiness for a day - go fishing.

If you want happiness for a month - get married.
If you want happiness for a year - inherit a fortune.
If you want happiness for a lifetime - help someone else.
If you want happiness for eternity - know yourself.

-Chinese Proverb

Where there is no vision, the people perish.

-Proverbs 29:18

If you treat people to a vision of themselves, if you apparently
overrate them, you help them become what they are capable of
becoming. You know, if we take people as they are, we make
them worse. If we take them as they should be, we help them
become what they can be.

-Viktor Frankl

The will of a person committed to a larger purpose is a cry from
the soul that has been shaken and awakened. I do not know of a
single person who has made a worthwhile discovery or invention
who has not experienced a spiritual power.

- Kazuo Inamori
CEO, Matsushita Corporation

I observed that in exceptional teams the task was no longer
separate from the self… but rather identified with this task so
strongly that you could not define his real self without including
that task.

-Abraham Maslow

People do not focus on the long term because they have to but because they want to.

-Peter Senge

Author, The Fifth Discipline

Fail to honor people, they will fail to honor you. But of a great leader, when his work is done, his aim fulfilled, the people will say, "We did this ourselves."

-Lao-tzu

CHARACTERISTICS CRITICAL TO SURVIVING AND THRIVING

- *Being able to make up your mind*
- *Being able to improvise*
- *Being able to live with your decisions*
- *Being adaptable, making a good thing out of a bad thing*
- *Being able to remain calm, cool, and collected*
- *Being able to hope for the best while preparing for the worst*
- *Being able to understand and influence other people*
- *Being able to control psychological fear*
- *Being able to exercise patience*

-Team Trek

Consider it a sheer gift, friends, when tests and challenges come at you from all sides. You know that under pressure, your faith life is forced into the open and shows its true colors. So don't try to get out of anything prematurely. Let it do its work so you become mature and well developed.

-James 1

You cannot teach a man anything; you can only help him to find it within himself.

-Galileo Galilei

A WELL-LIVED LIFE, FROM II TIMOTHY

- *Pray about everything*
- *Live simply in humility and contemplation*
- *Love God and others*
- *Mature in faith*
- *Guard your reputation*
- *Remain cool and collected*
- *Be accessible and hospitable*
- *Stay balanced in consumption of food and drink*
- *Be gentle and not thin-skinned*
- *Exercise daily in God*
- *Model the way for others*
- *Care for family members*
- *Pursue a life of love, wonder, faith, steadiness, and courtesy*
- *Seize life's opportunities*
- *Grow rich in helping others*

We exult in our tribulations, knowing that tribulation brings about perseverance, and perseverance, proven character, and proven character, hope.

-Romans 5:3-4

No one can make you feel inferior without your consent.

-Eleanor Roosevelt

DUTY, HONOR, COUNTRY

Have a heart that is clean
A vision that is great
Proud and unbending in honest failure
Humble and gentle in success
Not substituting words for action
Not seeking the path of comfort
Face the stress of difficulty and challenge
Learn to stand up in the storm
Have compassion on those who fail
Master yourself before you
  seek to master others
Learn to laugh but never forget how to weep
Reach into the future
  but do not neglect the past
Be serious but do not take yourself
  too seriously
Be modest so you will remember the
  simplicity of true greatness
Develop the open mind of true wisdom
The meekness of true strength.

-General Douglas MacArthur
(paraphrased from an address delivered
at West Point on May 12, 1962)

In a time of drastic change it is the learners who inherit the
future. The learned find themselves equipped to live in a world
that no longer exists.

-Eric Hoffer

*The reason why rivers and seas receive the homage of a hundred
mountain streams is that they keep below them. Thus they are
able to reign over all the mountain streams. So the sage, wishing
to be above men, places himself before them; wishing to be before
them, he places himself behind them. Though his place is above
men, they do not feel his weight; though his place is before them,
they do not count it an injury.*

-Lao-tzu

*Action seems to follow feeling, but really action and feeling go
together; and by regulating the action, which is under more direct
control of the will, we can indirectly regulate the feeling, which is
not.*

-William James
Philosopher

*I consider my ability to arouse enthusiasm among my people the
greatest asset I possess, and the way to develop the best that is in
a person is through appreciation and encouragement.*

-Charles Schwab
Former CEO, U.S. Steel Corporation

*I shall pass this way but once; any good therefore, that I can do
or any kindness that I can show to any human being, let me do it
now. Let me not defer nor neglect it, for I shall not pass this way
again.*

-Unknown

*The path of mastery is built on unrelenting practice, but it's also
a place of adventure ... whether it's a sport or an art or some*

other work, those we call masters are shamelessly enthusiastic about their calling ... those on the path of mastery are willing to take chances, play the fool ... The most powerful learning is that which is most like play.

-George Leonard

Author

Do all things without grumbling or disputing; that you may prove yourselves to be blameless and innocent, children of God above reproach in the midst of a crooked generation, among whom you appear as lights in the world.

-Philippines 2:14-15

If any man is able to convince me and show me that I do not think or act right, I will gladly change; for I seek the truth, by which no man was ever injured. But he is injured who abides in his error and ignorance.

-Marcus Aurelius

Learning does not mean acquiring more information; but expending the ability to produce the results we truly want in life.

-Peter Senge

If you come to me with your fists doubled, I think I can promise you that mine will double as fast as yours; but if you come to me and say, "Let us sit down and take counsel together, and, if we differ from one another, just what the points at issue are," we will presently find that we are not so far apart after all, that the points on which we differ are few and the points on which we agree are many and that if we only have the patience and the candor and the desire to get together, we will get together.

-Woodrow Wilson

If you want an enemy, then excel your friends; but if you want friends, let your friends excel you.

-L.L. Rochet Foucauld
French Philosopher

"Come to the edge," he said.
The people answered, "We are afraid."
"Come to the edge," he said.
The people answered, "We are afraid."
"Come to the edge," he said.
They came.
He pushed, and they flew.

-Guillaume Appollinaire

The happiness of your life depends upon the quality of your thoughts.

-Marcus Aurelius

There is only one way to happiness and that is to cease worrying about the things which are beyond the power of our will.

-Epictetus

It is in the nature of moral qualities that they are destroyed by deficiency and excess, just as we can see ... in the case of health and strength. For both excessive and insufficient exercise destroys ones strength, and both eating and drinking too much or too little destroy health, whereas the right quantity produces, increases, and preserves it. So it is with temperance, courage, and the other virtues. The man who shuns and fears everything and stands up to nothing becomes a coward, the man who is afraid of nothing, but marches up to every danger, becomes foolhardy.

-Aristotle

GEORGE WASHINGTON'S "RULES OF CIVILITY"

1. Every action in company ought to be with some sign of respect to those present.
2. In the presence of others sing not to yourself with a humming voice, nor drum with your fingers or feet.
3. Speak not when others speak, sit not when others stand, and walk not when others stop.
4. Turn not your back to others, especially in speaking; jog not the table or desk on which another reads or writes; lean not on anyone.
5. Be no flatterer, neither play with anyone that delights not to be played with.
6. Read no letters, books, or papers in company; but when there is a necessity for doing it, you must ask leave. Come not near the books or writing of anyone so as to read them unasked; also look not nigh when another is writing a letter.
7. Let your countenance be pleasant, but in serious matters somewhat grave.
8. Show not yourself glad at the misfortune of another, though he were your enemy.
9. They that are in dignity or office have in all places precedency, but whilst they are young, they ought to respect those that are their equals in birth or other qualities, though they have no public charge.

10. It is good manners to prefer them to whom we speak before ourselves, especially if they be above us, with whom in no sort we ought to begin.

11. Let your discourse with men of business be short and comprehensive.

12. In visiting the sick do not presently play the physician if you be not knowing therein.

13. In writing or speaking give to every person his due title according to his degree and custom of the place.

14. Strive not with your superiors in argument, but always submit your judgment to others with modesty.

15. Undertake not to teach your equal in the art he himself professes; it savors of arrogancy.

16. When a man does all he can, though it succeeds not well, blame not him that did it.

17. Being to advise or reprehend anyone, consider whether it ought to be in public or in private, presently or at some other time, also in what terms to do it; and in reproving show no sign of choler, but do it with sweetness and mildness.

18. Mock not nor jest at anything of importance; break no jests that are sharp or biting; and if you deliver anything witty or pleasant, abstain from laughing thereat yourself.

19. Wherein you reprove another be unblamable yourself, for example is more prevalent than precept.

20. Use no reproachful language against anyone, neither curses nor revilings.

21. Be not hasty to believe flying reports to the disparagement of anyone.

22. Let your apparel be modest, and endeavor to accommodate nature rather than procure admiration. Keep to the fashion of your equals, such as are civil and orderly with respect to time and place.

23. Play not the peacock, looking everywhere about you to see if you be well decked, if your shoes fit well, if your stockings set neatly and

clothes handsomely.

24. Associate yourself with men of good quality, esteem your own reputation, for it is better to be alone than in bad company.

25. Let your conversation be without malice or envy, for it is a sign of tractable and commendable nature; and in all causes of passion admit reason to govern.

26. Be not immodest in urging your friend to discover a secret.

27. Utter not base and frivolous things amongst grown and learned men, nor very difficult questions or subjects amongst the ignorant, not things hard to be believed.

28. Speak not of doleful things in time of mirth nor at the table; speak not of melancholy things, as death and wounds; and if others mention them, change, if you can, the discourse. Tell not your dreams but to your intimate friends.

29. Break not a jest when none take pleasure in mirth. Laugh not aloud, not at all without occasion. Deride no man's misfortunes, though there seem to be some cause.

30. Speak not injurious words, neither in jest or earnest. Scoff at none, although they give occasion.

31. Be not forward, but friendly and courteous, the first to salute, hear and answer, and be not pensive when it is time to converse.

32. Detract not from others, but neither be excessive in commending.

33. Go not thither where you know not whether you shall be welcome or not. Give not advise without being asked; and when desired, do it briefly.

34. If two contend together, take not the part of either unconstrained, and be not obstinate in our opinion; in things indifferent be of the major side.

35. Reprehend not the imperfections of others, for that belongs to parents, masters, and superiors.

36. Gaze not on the marks or blemishes of others, and ask not how they

came. What you may speak in secret to your friend deliver not before others.

37. Speak not in an unknown tongue in company, but in your own language; and that as those of quality do, and not as the vulgar. Sublime matters treat seriously.

38. Think before you speak; pronounce not imperfectly nor bring out your words too hastily, but orderly and distinctly.

39. When another speaks, be attentive yourself, and disturb not the audience. If any hesitate in his words, help him not, nor prompt him without being desired; interrupt him not, nor answer him till his speech be ended.

40. Treat with men at fit times about business, and whisper not in the company of others.

41. Make no comparisons; and if any of the company be commended for any brave act of virtue, commend not another for the same.

42. Be not apt to relate news if you know not the truth thereof. In discoursing of things you have heard, name not your author always. A secret discover not.

43. Be not curious to know the affairs of others, neither approach to those that speak in private.

44. Undertake not what you cannot perform; but be careful to keep your promise.

45. When you deliver a matter, do it without passion and indiscretion, however mean the person may be you do it to.

46. When your superiors talk to anybody, hear them; neither speak nor laugh.

47. In disputes be not so desirous to overcome as not to give liberty to each one to deliver his opinion, and submit to the judgment of the major part, especially if they are judges of the dispute.

48. Be not tedious in discourse, make not many digressions, nor repeat

often the same matter of discourse.

49. Speak no evil of the absent, for it is injust.

50. Be not angry at table, whatever happens; and if you have reason to be so show it not; put on a cheerful countenance, especially if there be strangers, for good humor makes one dish a feast.

51. Set not yourself at the upper end of the table; but if it be your due, or the master of the house will have it so, contend not, lest you should trouble the company.

52. When you speak of God or his attributes, let it be seriously, in reverence and honor, and obey your natural parents.

53. Let your recreations be manful, not sinful.

54. Labor to keep alive in your breast that little spark of celestial fire called conscience.

BENJAMIN FRANKLIN, AUTOBIOGRAPHY, PLAN FOR MORAL PERFECTION

It was about this time I conceived the bold and arduous project of arriving at moral perfection. I wish'd to live without committing any fault at any time; I would conquer all that either natural inclination, custom, or company might lead me into. As I knew, or thought I knew, what was right and wrong, I did not see why I might not always do the one and avoid the other. But I soon found that I had undertaken a task of more difficulty than I had imagined. While my care was employ'd in guarding against one fault, I was often surprised by another; habit took the advantage of inattention; inclination was sometimes too strong for reason. I concluded, at length, that the mere speculative conviction that it was our interest to be completely virtuous, was not sufficient to prevent our slipping; and that the contrary habits must be broken, and good ones acquired and established, before we can have any dependence on a steady, uniform rectitude of conduct. For this purpose I therefore contrived the following method.

In the various enumeration's of the moral virtues I had met with in my reading, I found the catalogue more or less numerous, as different writers included more or fewer ideas under the same name. Temperance, for example, was by some confined to eating and drinking, while by others it was extended to mean the moderating every other pleasure, appetite, inclination, or passion, bodily or mental, even to our avarice and ambition. I propos'd to myself, for the sake of clearness, to use rather more names, with fewer ideas annex'd to each, than a few names with more ideas; and I included under thirteen names of virtues all that at that time occurr'd to me as necessary or desirable, and annexed to each a short precept, which fully express'd the extent I gave to its meaning.

These names of virtues, with their precepts, were:

1. TEMPERANCE.
  Eat not to dullness; drink not to elevation.

2. SILENCE.
  Speak not but what may benefit others or yourself; avoid trifling conversation.

3. ORDER.
  Let all your things have their places; let each part of your business have its time.

4. RESOLUTION.

Resolve to perform what you ought; perform without fail what
you resolve.

5. FRUGALITY.

Make no expense but to do good to others or yourself; i.e.,
waste nothing.

6. INDUSTRY.

Lose no time; be always employ'd in something useful; cut off
all unnecessary actions.

7. SINCERITY.

Use no hurtful deceit; think innocently and justly, and, if you
speak, speak accordingly.

8. JUSTICE.

Wrong none by doing injuries, or omitting the benefits that
are your duty.

9. MODERATION.

Avoid extremes; forbear resenting injuries so much as you think
they deserve.

10. CLEANLINESS.

Tolerate no uncleanliness in body, cloaths, or habitation.

11. TRANQUILITY.

Be not disturbed at trifles, or at accidents common or
unavoidable.

12. CHASTITY.

Rarely use venery but for health or offspring, never to dullness, weakness, or the injury of your own or another's peace or reputation.

13. HUMILITY.

Imitate Jesus and Socrates.

My intention being to acquire the habitude of all these virtues, I judg'd it would be well not to distract my attention by attempting the whole at once, but to fix it on one of them at a time; and, when I should be master of that, then to proceed to another, and so on, till I should have gone thro' the thirteen; and, as the previous acquisition of some might facilitate the acquisition of certain others, I arrang'd them with that view ...

I made a little book, in which I allotted a page for each of the virtues. I rul'd each page with red ink, so as to have seven columns, one for each day of the week, marking each column with a letter for the day. I cross'd these columns with thirteen red lines, marking the beginning of each line with the first letter of one of the virtues, on which line, and in its proper column, I might mark, by a little black spot, every fault I found upon examination to have been committed respecting that virtue upon that day. I determined to give a week's strict attention to each of the virtues successfully. Thus, in the first week, my great guard was to avoid every the least offence against Temperance, leaving the other virtues to their ordinary chance, only marking every evening the faults of the day. Thus, if in the first week I could keep my first line, marked T. clear of spots, I suppos'd the habit of that virtue so much strengthen'd, and its opposite weaken'd, that I might venture extending my attention to include the next, and for the following week keep both lines clear of spots. Proceeding thus to the last, I could go thro' a course complete in thirteen weeks and four courses in a year. And like him who, having a garden to weed, does not attempt to eradicate all the bad herbs at once, which would exceed his reach and strength, but works on one of the beds at a time, and having accomplish'd the first, proceeds to a second, so I should have, I hoped, the encouraging pleasure of seeing on my pages the progress I made in virtue, by clearing successively my lines of their spots, till in the end by a number of courses, I should be happy in viewing a clean book, after a thirteen weeks' daily examination.

TEMPERENCE

EAT NOT TO DULLNESS. DRINK NOT TO ELEVATION

	S	M	T	W	T	F	S
T							
S	●	●		●		●	
O	● ●	●	●		●	●	●
R			●				
F		●			●		
I			●				
S							
J							
M							
C							
T							
C							
H							

My scheme of ORDER gave me the most trouble; and I found that, tho' it might be practicable where a man's business was such as to leave him the disposition of his time, that of a journeyman printer, for instance, it was not possible to be exactly observed by a master, who must mix with the world, and often receive people of business at their own hours. Order, too, with regard to places for things, papers, etc., I found extremely difficult to acquire. I had not been early accustomed to it, and, having an exceedingly good memory, I was not so sensible of the inconvenience attending want of method. This article, therefore, cost me so much painful attention, and my faults in it vexed me so much, and I made so little progress in amendment, and had such frequent relapses, that I was almost ready to give up the attempt, and content myself with a faulty character in that respect, like the man who, in buying an ax of a smith, my neighbour, desired to have the whole of its surface as bright as the edge. The smith consented to grind it bright for him if he would turn the wheel; he turn'd, while the smith press'd the broad face of the ax hard and heavily on the stone, which made the turning of it very fatiguing. The man came every now and then from the wheel to see how the work went on, and at length would take his ax as it was, without farther grinding. "No," said the smith, "turn on, turn on; we shall have it bright by-and-by; as yet, it is only speckled." "Yes," says the man, "but I think I like a speckled ax best." And I believe this may have been the case with many, who, having, for want some such means as I employ'd, found the difficulty of obtaining good and breaking bad habit in other points of vice and virtue, have given up the struggle, and concluded that "a speckled ax was best"; for something, that pretended to be reason, was every now and then suggesting to me that such extreme nicety as I exacted of myself might be a kind of foppery in morals, which, if it were known, would make me ridiculous; that a perfect character might be attended with the inconvenience of being envied and hated; and that a benevolent man should allow a few faults in himself, to keep his friend in countenance.

In truth, I found myself incorrigible with respect to Order; and now I am grown old, and my memory bad, I feel very sensibly the want of it. But, on the whole, tho' I never arrived at the perfection I had been so ambitious of obtaining, but fell far short of it, yet I was, by the endeavour, a better and happier man than I otherwise should have been if I had not attempted it; as those who aim at perfect writing by imitating the engraved copies, tho's they never reach the wish'd for excellence of those copies, their hand is mended by the endeavour, and is tolerable while it continues fair and legible.

It may be well my posterity should be informed that to this little artifice, with the blessing of God, their ancestor ow'd the constant felicity of his life, down to his 79th year in which this is written.

Benjamin Franklin

SUGGESTED READINGS

The Holy Bible

Adversity Quotient by Paul G. Stoltz

Emotional Intelligence by Daniel Goleman

First Things First by Stephen R. Covey

Gift From The Sea by Anne Morrow Lindbergh

I'm No Hero by Charlie Plumb

Inside Out by Lawrence J. Crabb

Leaders by Warren G. Bennis

Locking Arms by Stu Weber

Machiavelli On Modern Leadership by Arthur Ledeen

Man's Search For Meaning by Viktor E. Frankl

Poor Richard's Almanac by Benjamin Franklin

Principle Centered Leadership by Stephen R. Covey

Servant Leadership by Robert K. Greenleaf

Seven Habits Of Highly Effective People by Stephen R. Covey

Tender Warrior by Stu Weber

The Book Of Seven Truths by Calvin Miller

The Fifth Discipline by Peter M. Senge

The Leadership Challenge by James M. Kouzes & Barry Z. Posner

The Leadership Engine by Noel M. Tichy

The Moral Compass by William J. Bennett

The Power Principle by Blaine Lee & Stephen R. Covey

The Road Less Traveled by M. Scott Peck

The West Point Way of Leadership by Col. Larry R. Donnithorne (Ret.)

The Winning Attitude by John C. Maxwell

They Call Me Coach by John R. Wooden

The Wisdom of Wolves by Twyman L. Towery, Ph.D.

SUGGESTED FILMS

12 O'clock High

Apollo 13

Braveheart

Castaway

Chariots Of Fire

Dead Poets Society

Field Of Dreams

First Knight

Forrest Gump

Ghandi

Gladiator

Glory

Groundhog Day

Henry V

High Noon

Hoosiers

It's A Wonderful Life

Joan Of Arc

Mr. Smith Goes To Washington

Remember The Titans

Rudy

The Edge

Twelve Angry Men

ABOUT TEAM TREK

Team Trek is an organization whose mission it is to build people and connect teams through unique experiential learning methods. To this end, it was founded in 1994 by Gary Gore in Memphis, Tennessee, and continues to maintain its headquarters there. The Team Trek Learning Center is located on 800 beautiful and rugged acres situated near Greer's Ferry Lake, Heber Springs, Arkansas.

Team Trek offers its clients a variety of services, including team interventions conducted both at Heber Springs and on-site at client locations. Pre-intervention assessment, post-intervention follow-up, 360-degree feedback surveys, personality-preference sorters, and coaching are offered to round out its client offerings. Team Trek has frequently been called "The Disney World of experiential learning." Each year, it reaches thousands of people to further its mission.

For more information on Team Trek, call client services at (901) 767-0334, e-mail teamtrek@teamtrek.com, or visit their Web site at www.teamtrek.com. They can be reached by mail at 500 E. Racquet Club Place, Memphis, Tennessee 38117.

Building people, connecting teams